Court in

Crime and policing in WWII Hastings

Written and compiled
by Victoria Seymour

Foreword by Ann Widdecombe M.P.

First published in 2004
By Victoria Seymour

Copyright Victoria Seymour.

Email: mail@victoriaseymour.com
Website: www.victoriaseymour.com

ISBN: 09543901-2-1

A catalogue record for this book is available from the British Library.

Printed in Great Britain by

impression IT.
26, Brunel Road
St Leonards on Sea,
East Sussex
TN38 9RT
www.impressionit.co.uk

Court in the Act is dedicated to:

The Hastings and St Leonards WWII Police Force and Magistrates.

My sincere gratitude goes to all those who contributed their WWII memories and professional knowledge to this book:

Ex-Inspector Charles Banks, Ex-Inspector Sidney Thompson, Ex-Inspector Maxwell Judge, Ex-Detective Sergeant Reginald Fowler, Ex-Constable Cecil Manklow, Ex-Constable Kenneth Buddle.

Photographs of the past and present day police force were supplied by courtesy of Police Superintendent Dick Barton. Advice and information on modern magistrates' court procedure and police statistics were given by Detective Constable Sophie McGarel and Andrew Mowle, Finance and Administration Manager, Paul Edwards, Acting Divisional Legal Manager, Eastern Sussex Magistrates' Courts. Thanks for advice on past and present magistrate courts are due to Leslie Adams, Former Deputy Clerk to the Justices, Michael Chaloner JP, and Margery Lister JP and the Magistrates' Association.

Personal memories were recounted by Hastings and St Leonards Residents: Miss Joyce Brewer, Mr Ivor White, Miss Stella Francis, Mr Noel Care, Mrs Yvonne Thornley, Mr Ivor Thornely, Mrs Jean Gill, Mrs Marjorie Nunn, Mrs P Jones, Mrs P Dann, Mrs K Vaughan, Mrs E Hammond, Mrs Elaine Wiltshire, Mrs Violet Manklow and family historian Mr Ronald Burkin.

My thanks to The Hastings and St. Leonards Observer for permission to use archive news items and images, to the staff of Hastings Reference Library for their excellent assistance, to Hastings Museum for images and information, to the Imperial War Museum for photographs and posters, to Barbara Brocchi for additional photography and to Wendy Johnson for her valuable help with the final stages of this book

ALSO BY THE SAME AUTHOR:

Letters to Hannah ~ WWII Recollections of Hastings and South East England.

Letters from Lavender Cottage ~ Hastings in WWII and Austerity

Foreword

This is a very entertaining and informative book which will increase our knowledge of policing and everyday life in Britain in the Second World War. It paints a picture of a society that was on the whole obedient to the authorities at a time of severe national emergency but which was liberally peppered with people who were determined to take advantage of the situation. The methods of policing at a time of an immense increase in law are fascinatingly described.

At first sight a month in prison for allowing a light to escape from behind a curtain might look like something more appropriate for the Victorian age than for the middle of the twentieth century but, in fact, the regulation in question, like many others, preserved lives. Victoria Seymour is to be congratulated on the detail of her research but for all that the book is an easy read.

Miss Ann Widdecombe. M P

SETTING THE SCENE

Hastings' original Magistrates' Court and Town Hall, now a museum was built in 1823 in the Old Town's High Street. In 1836, the Watch Committee, the body appointed by the government, established a

The 1854 Police Force outside the High Street Police Station

formal police force and the Old Town Hall thenceforth became the first police station, with a complement of one inspector, three sergeants and nine constables. At that time, the population of Hastings was about eight thousand. By the mid-1870s, a rapidly expanding town and population created a need for a larger magistrates' court and municipal building so a new town hall was proposed. It was agreed to hold a national competition for a design, with a prize of £100 for the winner. Thirty-six entries were received and a grandiose design by Messrs Cross, Jeffery, Skiller and Wells was the winner. For unknown reasons, the original plan was rejected and in 1878 the council accepted a design by Henry

The former courthouse and police station, now a museum

1

The Queen's Road Town Hall side and rear views

Illustrated London News drawing of Mayor W. F. Revill and guests at the Town Hall opening, 1881

Ward, which it was estimated would cost £15,000. A tender submitted by D G Jones of Gloucester for £12,180 was accepted and building work began on the Queen's Road site in 1880.

According to local press reports of the day, some thought the new building's gothic lines, formal stone exterior and stained-glass windows were heavy and chapel-like. Others found it handsome, even imposing. The interior, with a grand, first floor council chamber and committee rooms, was elegantly furbished; in this part of the building almost all of the original features are intact. It is pleasing to note that in 1999, in spite of its Victorian critics, Hastings Town Hall was added to the Statutory List of Buildings of Special Architectural Interest.

The foundation stone for the building was laid by Mayor Henry Winter on the 24th March 1880. To celebrate the occasion a formal luncheon was held at the Claremont Institute, now Hastings Public Library. The completed building was officially declared open by Hastings' Mayor, on 7th of September 1881 at 1.20pm: "As cloudy and threatening skies gave way to sunshine of unclouded brilliance". A luncheon was held in a marquee, set up on the adjoining cricket ground, now the Priory

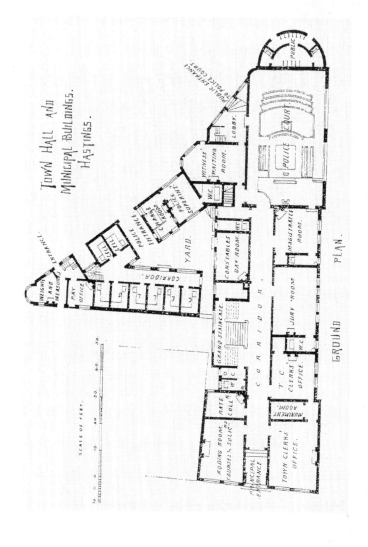

Original Ground Plan of the Queen's Road Town Hall, Court and Police Station

Meadow Shopping Centre. A quote from the 1881 Hastings and St Leonards Chronicle displays a pithiness not seen in today's local press reporting: "The speeches at the luncheon were not of that inordinate length, which all too often distinguishes utterances at ceremonies of a public character". An evening reception was held in the Town Hall for 500 people, with a concert of musical recitals and songs that was followed by a grand ball. The office of magistrate was then, as now, a voluntary undertaking and the lay magistrate in the judicial system of England and Wales has an ancient history. It can be traced back to the year 1195, when Richard I commissioned certain knights to preserve the peace in unruly areas. They were responsible to the king for ensuring that the law was upheld; they preserved the 'King's Peace' and were known as Keepers of the Peace. The present title Justices of the Peace has existed since 1361. For the following 600 years, and up until today, Justices of the Peace have undertaken the greater part of the judicial work carried out in England and Wales and they still retain the power to bind over unruly persons to be of good behaviour. Before 1835, justices in towns were appointed in accordance with rights granted by charter. The Municipal Corporations Act 1835 provided for them to be nominated by the Lord Chancellor for the boroughs, in consultation with local advisers. The system of appointment, which led to a preponderance of Conservatives on the benches, was challenged by the Liberal Government in 1906. The property-owning qualification was abolished for county magistrates and the Royal Commission on the Appointment of Justices of the Peace in 1910 recommended the institution of an advisory committee system and a few years later the boroughs had also formed such committees. It was not until The Sex Disqualification (Removal) Act 1919 came into force on 23rd December 1919 that women became magistrates.

Upper room of the Hastings Central Station, 1912

5

The first woman magistrate, Mrs. Ada Summers, Mayor of Stalybridge, an active suffragist, was sworn in on 31 December 1919. At that time, mayors of boroughs became justices, as well as taking the role the chairmen of borough benches, by right of office. Mrs. Summers was therefore probably the first woman also to adjudicate in court. On 1 January 1920, at least six women were appointed magistrates and by 1929 all county benches included at least one woman, although 55 borough benches were all male. By 1942 only nine divisions were without a woman magistrate. By 1947 the Magistrates' Association recommended to the Royal Commission of Justices of the Peace that immediate steps be taken to ensure all benches had adequate numbers of women magistrates.

The new Hastings Magistrates' Court was said to be, "one of the largest in the country and fitted up with every necessary accommodation". The walls and ceilings of the police court were clad in dark oak, creating a forbidding atmosphere. It was this courtroom that became the scene of the cases brought before the magistrates in WWII. In August 1929, it was reported in the Hastings and St Leonards Observer that: " A tasteful addition to the sombre interior of the court at the town hall has been completed, in the form of a series of escutcheons, emblazoned by Colonel F G Langham and his son Mr R H Langham. The various coats of arms, which are painted on oak panels behind the magistrates' seats, provide a welcome splash of colour". It would seem from local memory that Colonel Langham

Hastings Central Police Station flooded, 1913

6

himself provided a welcome splash colour to the court. He was a WWI war hero, of the Royal Sussex Regiment and it was said of him that he used to walk about no-man's land, waving a walking stick and cheering on his men. When Colonel Langham resumed his career in the legal profession he lived at Battle and travelled to Hastings by bus, in the company of his black Labrador, Jack, who would snooze under his master's desk during office hours.

Today, the exterior design of the Town Hall appears little altered, apart from the absence of the original decorative chimneys, which were demolished in 1959. Some of the exterior stonework friezes were also removed and placed in storage. It is on the ground floor interior where the most changes have taken place. The former robing, jury and magistrates' rooms are now council offices and the magistrates' court has become Hastings Information Centre. All that remains of the original oak panelling of the court is the ceiling and the public gallery, which is now office accommodation. On the ground floor of the new building and connected to the Magistrates' Court was Hastings Central Police Station. The larger rooms of the police station are now also offices and the former prison cells are used variously for the storage of official records, as a boiler room and as wardrobe space for councillors' ceremonial robes. The police cells were used only for overnight prisoners, those awaiting appearances in court or for transfer to penal institutions. The cells on the ground floor were for male prisoners and those above for female. The small yard in the centre of the buildings was used for prisoner's exercise. At the foot of the stairs that lead to the former public gallery there remains a very small, triangular cupboard-like room with a door that is perforated at the top; this was used as a detention room. There was also a public urinal situated in this section of the building. The figure-four design of the building is considered to be clever use of an awkward site. The town hall was built on the edge of water meadows, which are below sea level. Here, the monks from a 12th century priory, which gave its name to the spot, tended their cattle. In spite of a modern drainage system, flooding of this area occasionally occurs to a minor extent even today. It was certainly frequent enough during the earlier part of the 20th century to cause considerable inconvenience to the police premises, as recalled by Jean Gill, (nee Griffen), who started work at the Town Hall Magistrates' Court in 1948, at the age of 16. She was primarily

1921. Hastings Police Mounted Section.
Left to right :- P.Cs. Milton, Lavender, Funnell, Taylor and Wood.

8

Crown Inspection — 6th May, 1936. Lt. Col. Allan, H.M. Inspector of Constabulary, Mr. J. Bell, Chief Constable, and Superintendent W. J. Buddle. Standing beside the motor cycles are P.Cs. Dann and Parsons, and Detective Constable Carter.

1936. The first motor cars used by Hastings County Borough Police. Drivers :- P.Cs. E. Metcalf and W. Erridge.

1938. The Special Constabulary parading for the first time in uniform, under Major E. H. Langham. T.D., (Commandant).

11

employed as a secretary to the Clerks of the Justices and worked in the Middle Street law offices, close to the town hall. These offices were flooded about four times a year and always in the first week in August; a phenomenon connected to tides. Jean Gill remembers working at her desk, as water welled up through the floorboards and rose round her ankles. Phoning Inspector Banks in desperation she was told there was no need to worry until the water reached her knees! Later, a faucet was installed in the office, so that as the waters subsided the floors could be hosed down and the sewage sludge could be washed away with the retreating tide. Because of the flooding, the bottom drawers of filing cabinets were never used and a supply of Wellington boots was kept in the office for flood emergencies.

Among the contributors to this book are four former police officers, three of whom served in The Hastings County Borough Police Force before and during WWII. They have provided details that have brought to life the factual reports of wartime magistrates' courts and memories of a style of policing that has now passed. These contributors are:

Ex-Inspector Charles Banks, aged 91, the son of a Metropolitan Police Officer; he joined Hastings police force in 1932. Many of the police officers and court officials mentioned in this book were well known to him.

Ex-Inspector Sidney Thompson, aged 92, joined Hastings Police Force in 1934; he was interviewed for the job by Chief of Police Joseph Bell, along with 11 other applicants and was among the four accepted.

Ex-Police Constable Cecil Manklow, aged 91, joined the Hastings Police Force in 1934. This was the period of the depression and mass unemployment and Cecil had 10 different jobs in the few years leading up to his applying to join the force. He said that his police enrolment medical examination took place in the Central Police Station and was carried out by the police surgeon, Doctor Field: "It was a bitterly cold day in February and we had to strip off, with no heating in the room. I remember that a police dog, an Alsatian, was also present during the medical".

Ex-Police Constable Kenneth Buddle, aged 80, joined Hastings Police force in 1946. His father, grandfather and a cousin were police officers in Ramsgate and Ken is a cousin to Superintendent Buddle, who served in the Hastings Police Force until his retirement in 1944.

ACT ONE 1939

One of the major burdens that fell on British home front citizens in WWII was that of wartime, emergency legislation: The new laws brought before the magistrates' courts thousands of people who had previously been law-abiding citizens; the war also gave the criminal element new opportunities. If one were to believe the plots of the popular television series, Foyle's War, set in wartime Hastings, murder occurred there on a regular basis but in fact the rate of crimes of violence in the town was quite low during the war. The most common convictions were for breaches of the laws concerning blackout, looting, the curfew, restricted areas, the carrying of an identity card and for the flouting of regulations relating to the rationing of food and other goods and for the abuse of supplies. To list every instance of crime that occurred in wartime Hastings would make tedious reading; those selected are mostly first cases and provide a general view of the nature of offences. The names of defendants have been deliberately excluded but they can be found in the archive of the Hastings and St Leonards Observer, which is the source of most of the magistrate courts reports herein. Some of the cases that appeared in the newspaper were not followed through to their conclusion, possibly due to lack of column space or that presumed lack of public interest caused the stories to be dropped. Other, non-war related cases are included because they are sufficiently remarkable to deserve mention.

The pre-war police force played a major role in helping to form and organize the various WWII civil defence bodies in preparation for war, as well as continuing to fulfill their duty of protecting life and property and maintaining public order. The Special Constabulary was reorganized in 1938; a Police War Reserve Force was also established and all members were provided with a uniform for the first time. On the 1st January 1939, the first civilian staff was appointed; a shorthand typist and two telephone operators. When it seemed that war with Germany was inevitable, the Hastings Chief Constable ordered intensified training and the Police Headquarters and ARP Control Centre were duplicated, in case the main building was put out of action. Ex-Inspector Banks played a significant part in setting up an Air Raid Precautions Control Centre, organizing the installation of telephone lines and stationery in premises in Waldegrave Street, off Queen's Road. There was also an emergency HQ in Stone Court,

Gillsmans Hill. The exteriors of police stations, along with other important public buildings, were protected from the effects of blast by walls of sand bags and the telephone at the Hastings Central Police Station was moved to safer quarters. The familiar blue lamp that hung outside all police stations was extinguished, to comply with wartime blackout regulations. The interior of the police station was shored up with wooden props and the ceilings under-slung with wire mesh, in case they collapsed during an air raid. The police force took over the entire town hall and in its central, ground floor corridor an air raid shelter for 20 people was built from tree trunks and concrete.

Hastings Corporation set up a war emergency committee, to be overseen by the Chief of Police, the Town Clerk and Councillor Goldman, who were empowered to act as a war council to make decisions on emergency arrangements and expenditure. The police established a war emergency unit, to liaise with the military on matters relating to the billeting or movement of troops. For the duration of the war, Hastings Corporation moved its offices and chambers from the town hall to a boys' school, Summerfields House, a former Regency

Town Hall interior shelter under construction

mansion, set in parkland just beyond the town centre.

On Saturday July 8th 1939, Hastings held a blackout exercise and the local police and nearly 2000 voluntary ARP workers took part. The total blackout gave an opportunity to experiment with an "invisible policeman". The officer on duty at the town centre's Albert Memorial wore a coat and tin helmet that were treated with a special paint. The policeman could not be seen unless he stepped into the rays from nearby ultra-violet lamps but he would still remain invisible from the air.

At the outbreak of WWII, the structure of police forces was totally different from todays force. Most towns and even the smallest county had its own police force; there were 58 county forces and 121 borough or city forces, compared with about 40 today. In each locality the police officers were known to most of its inhabitants. The police service was run along similar lines to the armed forces. The working hours made huge demands on the individual; technically, a police officer was expected to work only an eight-hour day but he was on call for 24 hours every day and no overtime was paid for extra duties. Even

The 'invisible policeman' on duty

the time off in lieu was seldom available. There were no specialists in particular types of crime and the low numbers of police meant that during times of public disorder one force was expected to loan members to another. By 1940 the number of police officers in the country was down to 57,000, as younger men left the force to join the armed services. By 1941 the regular officers had been increased by the influx of 37,000 special constables and police war reserves. Ex-Inspector Banks described these men as a Godsend.

PC Manklow said that during the war the police were never really off duty: "If it was a rest day and the air raid siren went I had to get myself to the nearest police station, Clive Vale in my case. This applied to both day and night. If there was a bomb incident near where you were on duty, you had to go to the scene and take charge. All the emergency services had to refer to the police officer who was present, for co-ordination in rescue and recovery." In August 1939 Hastings Police were issued with service respirators and a blue painted, steel helmet, with the word POLICE inscribed on it in white paint. To prepare for war, the police and specials constables were trained in basic firefighting and giving advice on the reinforcement of the cellars of large buildings, for use as air raid shelters. The police force of the day was held in high esteem by the public and this aided them in operating during home front emergencies, an advantage that would have been invaluable in the event of a German invasion. The police also played a leading part in enforcing new and unpopular regulations on the home front. The now demolished Clive Vale Police Station, to which Ex-Constable Manklow refers, is recalled by Jean Gill. Her father, Ted Griffen, kept a second hand and antique furniture shop at Mount Road, very close to the Clive Vale Police Station, which was adjoined by two police houses, the fire station and a Hastings Corporation works yard. Along with these there stood a community of shops, some of which are still in business today. The dairy was owned by Ivor Thornely's father Bob, who was a part-time National Fire Serviceman. The dairy supplied the police station and frequently served Superintendent George Knell, who lived close to the police station and Detective Sergeant Pike, who occupied one of the two police houses. The police station was central to this tightly knit little community; both Jean Gill and Ivor Thornely mentioned that it had several prison cells for overnight detention and there was also additional accommodation, to house boys on remand, who were awaiting admission to an approved school. Being set on high ground,

Ted Griffen, with the Clive Vale Police houses in the background

the police station roof was a perfect location for fire watching; Ex-Constable Manklow said that he saw the flashes of the anti-aircraft guns on the cliffs at Dover, during bombing raids.

At the outbreak of war and until proper air raid sirens were installed, police officers in some areas would ride around on bicycles, blowing a whistle and wearing a placard that gave warning of approaching enemy aircraft. Later, sirens were hand cranked or electrically operated and initially installed on the roofs of police stations or officers' homes. These sirens needed a 24 hour presence to operate them. A gas attack was to be signalled by the use of hand turned rattles, a hundred year old device; hand bells would be rung when the danger had passed. Within days of the outbreak of war, the Hastings and St Leonards Observer was pleading for better and louder sirens; the sounds of those already in operation were either lost in the area's valleys or out to sea.

In early October 1939, Vigilant, who wrote the comment column, entitled "Flotsam and Jetsam", in the Hastings and St Leonards Observer, began a war-long campaign against those members of the community who he saw as failing to support the new regulations and the war effort generally. He took motorists to task for not maintaining their car gearboxes properly, conjecturing that the whining sounds they made as they laboured up Hastings' many steep hills could be mistaken for air raid sirens, thus alarming the public. One of Vigilant's favoured topics was the blackout regulations and soon he was asking: "Where are the police? The Air Raid Precaution Wardens are not being backed up by the police and up to the present time, no offender has been brought before the court for punishment". It was reported on September 23rd 1939 that a Hastings Observer journalist had walked round the town and found many windows insufficiently screened: "Marine Court was a blaze of lights that could be seen from Hastings Pier" (about a quarter of a mile distant). RAF pilots said that Hastings and St Leonards had the most lights showing on the coast and looked: "Like a fairyland at night".

Air raid siren situated at a police box

Vigilant was soon to be satisfied, when the first local offenders under the Lighting Restrictions Act appeared in Hastings' Magistrates' Court at the end of September. The cases were heard with the Mayor, Councillor Ford as Bench Chairman. He stated that the police had shown great patience but cases of carelessness and willful inattention were occurring. He reminded the offenders that the maximum penalty was a £100 fine or three months in prison but handed down fines of only one and two pounds. These sums may sound small by present reckoning but in 1939 £1 was equivalent to about £40 today. Some residents, who objected to being served a summons for flouting blackout regulations, approached the local magistrates in their own homes, to plead their case privately. Magistrates were easy to locate at that time as their home addresses were printed in a special section of the street directory; there were 36 magistrates in Hastings and St Leonards in 1939, including the Hastings Mayor.

The blackout conditions caused a huge rise in accidents, resulting in injury and deaths all over the country. Hastings, with its narrow alley ways, interspersed with random flights of steps and the high, unguarded pavements, posed a particular hazard and one night two special constables fell six feet from a pavement into the road; Special Constable C F Withers broke his right arm in the fall. The local criminal element took full advantage of the situation to commit offences under the cover of complete darkness and a number of handbag thefts and shop smash and grab burglaries occurred. A youth who stole a handbag from an elderly lady in the street was sent to a remand home, to await a vacancy in an approved school.

Local resident, Margery Nunn, recalls her own experiences with the problems of the blackout. She was married, aged 19, in 1939 and her first child was born in May 1940. She lived with her extended family in a Victorian house that overlooked Alexandra Park. Her 29 year-old bus driver husband, Cyril, was in a reserved occupation but he also served as a member of the Home Guard. He was additionally on permanent standby to transport troops, which he did on several occasions. Margery refused to be evacuated from Hastings with her baby, when the area came under the threat of invasion, as she could not face the prospect of being herded in a train, to an unknown destination, to what may have been unsuitable accommodation. She said her family was not the type that became afraid and panicked under pressure and she preferred to stay put. She spoke of her husband making and fitting the blackout blinds to cover the large windows of their home and said that it was a work of art putting them up at night and getting them down every morning. It was the lighting regulations that brought them their few contacts with the law; no matter how meticulous the blackout arrangements, there would always be one police officer or Air Raid Warden who would nit-pick. Householders were officially advised that during night raids they should leave their doors unlocked, in case the emergency services needed access, to administer first aid or carry out rescue work. One night, a police officer spotted a glimmer of light from one candle in the Nunn's bedroom and as his knocks on the front door did not wake the family, he entered the house, put his head round the bedroom door and ordered them to "put that light out".

In these days of wide-spread light pollution it is difficult to grasp the utter darkness that engulfed the country under blackout conditions. A compensation for the darkness was the view of the night sky, unhindered by reflected light. Margery said that due to the fear of having an accident, she hardly ever went out at night but she mentioned one occasion when she and her sister-in-law went on an after-dark escapade, in quest of chicken wire. The Headquarters of her husband's Home Guard Company was Bleaton House, a large residential property, nearby in Laton Road. This house was one of the many buildings commandeered for military purposes during the war. Margery's husband had noticed that in a garden shed at the HQ there was a long roll of wire mesh and as his family was planning to keep ducks in the garden, the wire mesh, already in short supply, was just what was needed. The Home Guard Commanding Officer gave permission for it to be removed and quickly, as the company was being moved to new quarters. Mr. Nunn was at work so the two ladies hastily set out in complete darkness, to search for the wire in the pitch dark shed and carry it home between them. On their return journey, they passed a police sergeant, who was on his way to liaise with the patrolling constable, posted opposite to the Home Guard HQ. Nothing was said by any party, as they passed each other in the blackness!

Vigilant had more to say on the matter of flouting lighting regulations, pointing out that in Germany the punishment for similar crimes was execution and that in Britain the miscreants should be brought before the judge at Assizes (now Crown Court). Vigilant pronounced that any person failing to observe the new blackout laws was: "A traitor in the community and helping the enemy as much as a German agent in our midst". In 1939, although Hastings was a popular, modern holiday resort, it still retained many of the attitudes of the small fishing village it had been for centuries; it was off the beaten track and almost like an island community in as much as strangers out of season were easily recognized. With the enemy, "just across the water", Hastings became obsessed with the idea of spies, fifth columnists and aliens. A man and woman, Jewish-German refugees from Austria, who applied for gas masks were questioned by the Chief Constable, who discovered that they were the guests of a local resident and so released. A foreign woman, a resident of Great Britain for 15 years, appeared before the Hastings Magistrates' Court in late September. The woman had changed her name on September 11th 1939 and had failed to notify the particulars to a registration officer. The magistrate issued a warning to foreigners that they must strictly comply with regulations under the Aliens Act. After the hearing, the woman was fortunate to have her case dismissed; the offence carried a fine of £100 or six months in prison. During WWII, thousands of foreigners in the UK were interned, which meant their being detained in communes for long periods, for no greater offence that that of not being British.

The carrying of gas masks by the public was never compulsory but Hastings' Chief Constable, Mr. J Bell, drew attention to the laxity in this matter. Cinemas tried to enforce their own terms of admission to the theatre, banning those who were not carrying gas masks. This caused indignation among the townspeople, who called it an interference with public liberty, as no such order had been issued for other places of entertainment and the carrying of a gas mask was a voluntary action. In the Armistice Day Parade in November 1939, certainly a bitter commemoration for those who had fought in the "war to end all wars", the police escort wore their respirators on parade for the first time.

The National Council of Women of Great Britain met at Hastings Town Hall in November under the chairmanship of Mrs. Johnson, to discuss the activities of the NCW during wartime. Hastings' only female police officer, Miss Joan E Edwards had been appointed in February 1937 but had since left the force and the position was vacant. Mrs. Johnson thought that to be in the position of being the only female police officer must be "dreadful" and that ten, not one female officers were needed at Hastings. She also referred to the plans for a Women's Auxiliary Police Force. Ex-Police Constable Manklow remembered Miss Edwards: "She was a reserved, well-educated upper class sort of woman. The men used to give her a hard time; making fun of her or just ignoring her. She left in the end".

10th November, 1939. Police escorting the Mayoral Divine Service procession.

By 1939, the Hastings Borough Police Force already had a record of charitable work, particularly for its administration of the police-aided clothing fund. In 1914, a Mr. Alfred Pett died at Hastings and left a legacy of £500 to Hastings Corporation: "To be invested and the interest therefrom to be used for the sole benefit of the deserving poor children of the town". Mr. Pett directed that the money was to be used for buying clothing, boots and food, whenever necessary. The will also laid down that the fund was to be administered by the Chief of Police of Hastings and his force, adding the hope that others would contribute to the fund. By 1931 the welfare work of the fund was well established: The Chief Constable's report to the Watch Committee stated that in 1930 it had: "Provided 341 pairs of boots and shoes, 658 pairs of stockings and socks and 105 other garments, together with quantities of beef, bread and potatoes, coal and groceries". The total amount spent by the fund for that year was £210. In spite of food and clothing rationing and other severe shortages, the Hastings Police continued this beneficent work throughout WWII. Vouchers were issued to hard up families and a supply of clothing was kept at the police station for needy cases. For the first wartime Christmas members of the Hastings Police Recreation Club organized a party and the constables dressed-up as waiters, to serve and entertain 80 children: "Loud cheers heralded the arrival of Father Christmas, (Police Constable Goodsell), whose sleigh was drawn by PCs Gorring and Greer, dressed up as mustangs". Police Constable Goodsell was the Hastings Police Station assistant jailer, known as a good cricket player and something of a prankster. The standard joke he played on new, young police officers was decades old. Since 1864, a clock tower, The Albert Memorial, had stood in Hastings Town Centre. At the base of the tower was a small door and the new recruit was told that it was his job to go inside and wind the clock every night. He was presented with a large, ornate key and sent out on what was a futile errand, as the key did not even fit the clock tower door!" A story told by Ex-Inspector Thompson belies the image we have of the dignified, old-time policeman. He said: "On the outbreak of war all the stocks of fireworks in private hands and businesses were confiscated, put in the police station yard and doused with buckets of water. The fireworks were left there for some time and the ones on top must have dried out, because they went off one night, at about 10.00pm. Ex-Inspector Banks also recalled the incident and said that Sgt Cheal tried to deal with the blaze but it was beyond control and the town was treated to an impromptu firework display. Ex-Inspector Thompson said that he knew who had ignited the fireworks but declined to say. Police Constable Manklow was less reticent when telling the same story, he said: "It was Police Constable L A P Kitney who set off the fireworks, when he flicked a still smouldering cigarette end among them. He's no longer with us but I don't think he would mind me telling this now".

ACT TWO 1940

During the so-called phoney war, training for all the emergency services continued: Some of this took place at the Hastings Corporation Depot next to the Drill Hall at Bulverhythe, which is the scene of the dramatic picture of the marching police officers wearing respirators. Ex-Inspector Banks recalled that in the yard there was a

WWII police officers in training at the Bulverhythe Depot

mock-up of a bomb-wrecked house and the police and war emergency services trained in its smoke-logged cellars and practised rescuing a dummy casualty. The gas training chamber was also on this site: Police Sergeant Frank Kemp was sent for a course in gas recognition and was provided with canisters of gas to teach the police and emergency workers how to identify the different odours. Ex-Inspector Thompson confirmed the location of the photograph, pointing out that the houses in the far left background were the railway cottages; he thought the gun in the lower left of the picture belonged to the navy. He remembered the times when police officers under training would put on yellow gas proof suits and masks and were sent to dig up the shingle on the beach, to prepare for carrying out rescues, while wearing the equipment. During the war, local police officers had firing practice in the sandpit at Fairlight and on the military ranges at Lydd, where they trained with service rifles and automatic weapons, to give the men the capability of dealing with German invaders or enemy airmen who had been shot down. Ex-Inspector Banks said that to re-enforce the police service, all retired, active police pensioners were re-called, to man the police sub-stations at Bohemia Road, The Ridge, Battle Road and Clive Vale.

Ex-Inspector Banks remembered the timetable for the sessions of the various Town Hall Courts: Daily sittings of the magistrates' court took place only if required; otherwise they were held on Tuesdays and Thursdays, from 10.30am onwards. The domestic court, at which the matters of affiliation, adoption and juveniles applying to marry were considered, was on Wednesday and the juvenile panel sat on Thursday afternoon. Assizes, Quarter Sessions and inquests also took place in the Town Hall Court but some inquests were held at St Helens Hospital (now demolished). When the court adjourned for lunch, the officials would often go the nearby Wellington Square's Castle Hotel (now demolished) or the Queens Hotel. Ex-Inspector Thompson said that as far as he knew, magistrates in WWII had no formal training as they do today. They were usually local people of note or business men, who were considered to be qualified for the bench by their life experience; they were guided in points of law then, as now, by the Clerk of the Court.

It was probably a misunderstanding about war emergencies that helped an offender to carry out the confidence trick that brought him to Hastings Police Court in January 1940. It was alleged, by a mother of five that the defendant, a trolley bus conductor, had told her that he was a member of the Secret Service and was working on the buses in order to get in touch with people he wished to meet. He was charged with obtaining £166 from the woman, on false pretences. Evidence was given by Detective Sergeant Stanley Copper, who said that when the warrant was read the accused denied the charge. The conductor had met the plaintiff's young son, while he was a passenger on the bus. He befriended the boy and "thinking him to be clever", took him to a wireless exhibition at Olympia and sometimes to church on Sunday mornings. The bus conductor told the mother that he owned land and property in Wales that he was well connected and had a good income. The mother disclosed her financial affairs to him and together they viewed properties in Hastings and St Leonards. These included the large residence, known as Castleham, at Hollington, which the accused persuaded the woman to try to buy jointly with him, for use as a boarding school and to provide a home and future for herself and her children. The mother opened a joint account with the accused and paid in £270 as a deposit, unaware that he had no money. The bus conductor admitted fraudulent representation and was bound over for three years, under the probation officer, on the condition that he entered a home to receive psychological treatment.

Vigilant had some words to say on an outbreak of slogan-scrawling mania by local fascists, adding that it was a waste of white paint, which could be put to better use on retouching the already-fading, blackout safety stripes, painted on curbstones, steps, lampposts and pillar boxes.

A flight of steps being painted for blackout safety

In wartime bill sticking continued to be illegal and in January 1940, under cover of the blackout, three men went out to stick bills on lampposts, street signs, walls and a church notice board, all the time followed by two special constables. The offence was compounded by the bill stickers flashing a torch, which could be seen in the sky above Falaise Road. It was not revealed exactly what information the bills conveyed but their distributors may have been members of the Right Club, a secret society founded by Archibald Ramsey in May 1939, to unify all the different right-wing groups in Britain. The club had a pro-German anti-Semitic influence. For the offence of bill sticking, the Falaise Road offenders were fined one pound each, plus 8/8d (44p) costs and one of the three was fined ten shillings (50p) for flashing a torch.

Although Britain had a good farming and manufacturing base at the start of WWII, it still needed to import millions of tons of food and other supplies. The country was very vulnerable to sea warfare and the Germans took full advantage of this, sinking hundreds of British merchant ships. It was this that led to the introduction of food and other rationing and opened the door to illegal and black market dealers. In order to combat this, the Ministry of Food employed inspectors,

Hi, what about a comma or something after my name?

sometimes called enforcers, to secretly observe how the new emergency regulations were being put into effect and to report on their findings. These inspectors were viewed with intense dislike even though they were doing important war work in trying to prevent Britain's reduced supplies being misused. The plainclothes enforcers, concealing their identity, would tell hard luck stories to retailers or restaurant owners, to subvert them into illegally supplying foodstuffs or meals. A successful prosecution by the Ministry of Food Inspector could result in a fine of up to £500, much more for a serious offence. A prison sentence could also be imposed.

Before food rationing commenced every person was obliged to register their custom with one retailer. When purchases were made, the retailer had to clip from the ration book the coupons appropriate to the date and food sold. The coupons had to tally with outgoings, to keep a check on the system and to enable the retailer to obtain repeat stock for registered customers. This nightmare of administration fell particularly heavily on small traders, who were sometimes not up to the job and so led to prosecutions of the technically innocent. Noel Care, who in the early part of WWII was a sixteen year-old grocery shop assistant in a small store in Cambridge Road, told of his experiences with rationing and shortages: "As the war progressed many things became scarce. The supplies of tinned food diminished; we kept ours for regular customers, as did most grocers. Biscuits became harder to get hold of, so when there were some in stock they were never put on display, a hint was just dropped to regular customers, but the shop only allowed a few ounces per customer; biscuits were sold loose in those days. The government ordered that everything was sold by weight and it became very difficult to explain to the older ladies that they could no longer ask for "three pennyworth of cheese" and that they could only have their ration, which had to be correctly weighed"

A Peek into the Past

What a fine fellow Custard Cream was, to be sure—a shortcake Biscuit sandwiched with delicious custard-flavoured cream! No wonder that Peek Frean's wartime biscuits are so good, with such an illustrious pre-war ancestry. These pre-war favourites will be back again after victory when zoning and limitation of supplies will be merely a memory.

BY APPOINTMENT TO

Peek Frean's

BRITAIN'S CRISPEST BISCUITS

H.M. KING GEORGE VI.   Made by Peek Frean & Co. Ltd., makers of famous biscuits

Vigilant returned to his rant against Light Restriction Order offenders: "The fines are not heavy enough…most of the incidents are just carelessness. Will only the occurrence of an actual air raid bring people to realize how necessary the regulations are? The police should be more vigilant, the Hastings' Magistrates should follow the example of those from Eastbourne, who impose bigger fines, of £5 to £20". It seemed that the worst blackout offenders were those who got up early and opened curtains or forgot the lights that were visible at the back of the house. In late January, a distant explosion at night had brought residents to their windows, opening blackout blinds and curtains to see if an air raid was in progress! A leader article in the Hastings and St Leonards Observer also expressed the view that the penalties for blackout offences were too trivial and convictions too few: "Air Raid Precaution Wardens ask, what is the use of reporting incidents, when only some of them are taken up by the police? The police say, what is the use of charging offenders when you know they will not be properly punished?" These remarks from 1940 have an uncomfortably contemporary ring to them.

Criminals continued to exploit the darkness: As dusk fell on a rainy February evening, an ATS girl (Auxiliary Territorial Service) was subjected to a vicious attack in St Margaret's Road. An assailant approached her from behind, grabbed her shoulder and attempted to wrench her handbag from her grasp. The girl kept hold of the bag and struck out at her attacker with her free hand. The thief hit the girl on the head and she fell, face down and unconscious, into the gutter, with cuts to her hands and face. The house surgeon at the Royal East Sussex Hospital said the injuries must have been made by an instrument of some kind. The man escaped with the bag, which contained 12/6d (63p). The unconscious girl was discovered some time later by a passerby. The victim was eventually able to identify her attacker and he was charged and arrested at his All Saints Road home, by Detective Sgt Stanley Copper. The Magistrate, Mayor Ford, committed the man for trial at Lewes Assizes. When the case came to court, the charge concerning the ATS girl was dropped, as she was too ill to attend but the accused was charged with robbing with violence two other women, at Ticehurst and Ramsgate. On passing sentence, Mr. Justice Humphrys said: "You are fortunate that you have not been tried for the additional case of robbery with violence, (referring to the ATS girl). The Medical Officer of the prison has declared you to be fit for corporal punishment and I should have felt bound to order you to receive the cat". The accused was given a sentence of 6 years penal servitude along with 18 months hard labour. The cat, or cat o'nine tails was a nine stranded whip that could inflict considerable pain and superficial lacerations. Flogging was abolished in 1962 and capital punishment three years later.

Before Hastings Police Court in March 1940 there appeared an 18 year old wife, the mother to a year old baby; her husband was in war service in the north of England. She was accused of unlawful use of premises. She had come to Hastings to look after her sick mother-in -law, who was subsequently taken into hospital. An older woman, who had been evacuated from London with her two year-old child, came to live with the young wife. The police watched the house for 9 consecutive nights and on all nights except two, the women brought men home. On the other nights the women were shadowed and as the police claimed: "Their conduct left little doubt as to their intentions". The police entered the premises on March 8th and found two men with the women, as well as the infants, who were in the same room. The police accepted that no money had changed hands and the two women were not seeking money. The police took the view that the younger woman was over-sexed and influenced by the older. When the 18 year old mother was sentenced to 3 months in prison she broke down and was led sobbing from the court. She appealed against her sentence but no report was made of the outcome of the appeal.

Digressing from his main bone of contention, Vigilant complained about the 9.00pm closing time that had been imposed on the Hastings public toilets during the first few weeks of the war. "Life is getting back to normal now; people are going out at night to entertainment. What impression will this early closure of public conveniences give to visitors?" Vigilant also began a personal crusade against Idle Talk, remarking on conversations about the postings of serving men, which he had overheard on the Hastings buses.

The first prosecution of the contravention of the Rationing Order appeared at Hastings Police Court in March: The charge was against the management of the St Leonards' branch of the grocery store, David Greig and one of its shop assistants. On 10th February 1940, the Food Control Inspector sent a member of his staff to buy some cooked ham and rashers of bacon from the store. In spite of a lecture on rationing regulations, given on the previous day, when the assistant served the undercover inspector he failed to ask him if he was registered at that shop and did not take the relevant coupons. It

CARELESS TALK
COSTS LIVES

should be remembered that the rationing system had only been in place for a few weeks and did not apply to every food; rashers of bacon were rationed but not cooked ham. The defending solicitor said that the offence took place in the middle of a very busy Saturday morning and the inspector had confused the shop assistant by asking for rationed and un-rationed goods at the same time. The magistrates decided to convict but as it was a first prosecution the fines imposed were deemed moderate; £1.00 on the shop assistant and £5.00 on the company. In a surprising show of frankness the inspector had admitted, during court proceedings, that he had subsequently eaten the ham and bacon! Offences against the Food rationing order often revealed shopkeepers who were more confused than criminal. Some of them were elderly or in poor health. The owner of a one-man shop in Hollington was partially disabled, as a result of action in the First World War and during a spell of illness he had to call on the help of a less-than-competent relative to help in the shop, which led to four Rationing Order offences being committed. In this case the shopkeeper was fined £4.00 with 14/- (70p) costs. Explanations and mitigating circumstances for an offence were hardly ever accepted by the court and fines were handed down almost as a matter of course.

The first local prosecution under the Defence Regulations Act was heard at Hastings Police Court in April 1940. A young man, who said he was a dress designer, was charged with attempting to take a photograph of an electricity pylon, without authority. The young man said he was unaware of the regulation and was seeking an artistic study of the wires against the sky and produced similar pre-war photographs as evidence; the young man was let off lightly with a fine of £2.00. Also in April, eighteen Lighting Restriction Order offenders appeared in the Police Court, The Chairman of the Bench, Mayor Ford, gave warning that if numbers did not decrease, future offenders would be dealt with more severely. He said that the fact that there had been no enemy air raids should not lead to public complacency. One of the offenders was an Air Raid Warden's wife, who said to the police constable when he came to her door. "Oh, my husband will be cross with me!" Vigilant received news of a forthcoming increase in blackout fines with the comment, "At long last!" During the next Magistrates' Court sitting bigger fines were imposed; £3 on one defendant and £2 on four others.

1940

The following case reveals the accepted, contemporary dress code for court appearances: Under the headline "Hatless Girl Rebuked", an eighteen year-old girl appeared before the Battle Bench charged with driving without a license and was fined £1.00 for the offence and reprimanded by the Chairman of the Bench for not wearing a hat in court. The address of the offender, possibly a domestic worker, was Normanhurst, the former, family home of Lady Brassey JP, who was also sitting on the Battle Bench that day. Normanhurst, demolished in 1957, was used later in WWII, to accommodate German Prisoners of War.

Vigilant turned his rhetoric to a new home front problem: "I have recently been receiving abusive letters from anti-war agitators, so I am pleased about the stern measure to be taken against the people who

A WWII German prisoner of war painted this impression of Normanhurst

have been carrying out anti-war work". The stern measure he was referring to was the extension of the death penalty, which could be imposed for the crimes of sabotage and spying. Due to a vigorous government campaign to alert the public, the possibility of spies was ever present in the public consciousness. In mid-May the police, armed with rifles and revolvers, were called out to the East Hill in response to a telephone call, reporting that a parachutist had been seen to descend in that area. The East Hill and the Firehills are a six mile stretch of fields, gorse and scrub, woodlands and cliff-tops, to the east of Hastings, which end at the isolated beaches of Pett Level. The "parachutist" proved to be a drifting and partly deflated barrage balloon, which passed by the town, a little out to sea. Barrage balloons were anchored to the ground by cables and equipped with fins, to keep them headed into the wind. They were positioned around likely bombing targets, to interfere with the flight paths of enemy aircraft. The barrage balloon's prime function was to force enemy aircraft to stay high, so placing them at the optimum height for engagement by anti-aircraft guns. Occasionally, one would escape anchor and drift away, dragging its cables over streets and roof tops.

Contemporary records show that the national suicide rate fell during

WWII. Until 1961, attempted suicide was a criminal offence in Great Britain and carried a prison sentence. The national trend did not seem to be reflected in the Hastings area in 1940, when suicides during that period were sadly frequent. Some suicide victims were unwilling service personnel, who possibly saw death as the only escape from their situation; others were grief-stricken people, whose family members had been killed in action. There were suicides of refugees, who either lived in the town or made the journey to the coast for the sole purpose of killing themselves. Such suicides seemed to increase after Dunkirk, when the threat of the invasion of Britain by the regime that the refugees had fled became very real. One such suicide, in late May 1940, was that of a 58 year old woman of German nationality and Jewish descent, who had come to Britain to escape Nazi oppression. She had secretly kept a supply of morphine tablets and a hypodermic syringe, because she feared her life might become unbearable. The German occupation of France had brought the enemy to within 22 miles, across the channel from Hastings. Due to the two-week delay reporting restrictions, Vigilant was able to say nothing in his column in early June about the evacuation from Dunkirk of over 338,000 members of the British European Forces. He just wrote a few words urging people to "Keep up their hearts". After the required two weeks

had elapsed, the people of Hastings and St Leonards were able to learn of the part played by local men in the Dunkirk Evacuation. Details of fatalities among the towns' servicemen were announced and the first military funeral took place, in the new Heroes' Corner, in Hastings Borough Cemetery. The soldier interred was Private Harry Victor Henham, aged 19, who died of wounds received on active service with the British Expeditionary Forces, as they retreated from Dunkirk.

Hastings residents were left in no doubt that war conditions now prevailed; the phoney war was over. All the evacuees, who had been brought to Hastings to seek safety from the expected bombing of towns and cities, were moved out. Evacuation for was quickly organized for much of the civilian population; the elderly, women, children and those considered as non-essential to the war-effort. This reduced the town's inhabitants from 65,000 to about 10,000. Police Constable Manklow's wife, Violet, and her four year-old son were among the young families who were hustled off to evacuation at a few hours' notice. She said: "There was no time to pack our bags properly, I had no money with me; well, we never had any spare money in the house in those days. We were sent to Bristol and as we arrived at our destination a raid was going on over the town and bits of debris were falling down from the railway station roof; Bristol wasn't safer than Hastings. It did not suit us being down there, you can't just turn up and start living with strangers in their house and expect it to be happy for everybody. So we came back to Hastings and set about bringing our whole family together, so that we could share things like rations and look after each other. Our neighbour was an old man who lived alone, so we made a gap in the fence so he could pop round to our house. He used to knock on our door when great formations of aircraft passed above Hastings, as he was frightened. He invariably asked, 'Are they ours?' My husband always said they were (even if they weren't) and because the answer came from a policeman the old man accepted this reply and felt happier". This attitude to the police illustrates the general opinion of the public to the wartime officers. Mrs Kathleen Vaughan of Hastings said: "They were very good men to have around. If you wanted to know anything you felt sure that if you asked a policeman you would get a sensible answer"

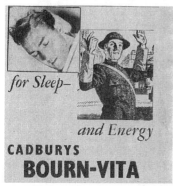

Their public status made police officers desirable advertising icons

A government billeting officer for evacuees was appointed in towns but in more sparsely populated places the job fell to a police officer or a volunteer, who might not be qualified for the sensitive task, other than by their position in the community. The evacuees' sometimes reluctant hosts were paid by the government; 10/6d (53p) for the first and 8/6d (43p) for each subsequent child. A mother and her baby came under a less than agreeable arrangement, that of lodgings only for a payment of 5/- (25p) for the mother and 3/- (15p) for the baby. The

Police officer escorts evacuees.

mother had to buy food and cook for herself and her child and this situation often led to bad feeling with the hosts. There were inevitably billeting payments frauds. Owing to the haste of the evacuation there were no serial numbers on forms and therefore no means of checking cases of deception. A Hastings' woman admitted that she had drawn money from the post office for the maintenance of two evacuees who were no longer with her. She was charged with obtaining money by false pretences in that she had drawn payments on sixteen occasions. A sentence of three months in prison was imposed.

A large number of aliens, including respected people who had resided or run a business in Hastings and St Leonards for years, were ordered 20 miles inland, to East Grinstead. In September 1939 there were over 71,000 registered enemy aliens in Britain. On the outbreak of war, the police arrested a large number of Germans living in Britain. The government feared that some of these people might be Nazi spies, pretending to be refugees. They were interned and held in various camps all over Britain. Like other refugees they eventually appeared before tribunals, which classified them into three different groups. 'A' class aliens were interned, whereas 'B' class aliens were allowed to leave the camps but had certain restrictions placed upon their movements. The majority of refugees were identified as 'C' class aliens and allowed to go free.

During this period of tension one of the leaders of Hastings Blackshirts, (Fascists) was described as being "detained", when he should have re-appeared in court for the non-payment of a fine.

The results of a pacifist overnight daubing exercise on a Hastings railway bridge parapet

Superintendent W. J. Buddle announced that the man was being held at Lewes Prison in connection with another matter. Five others, three women and two men, had also been detained under Emergency Regulations, by reason of their local, active association with the Fascist Movement. One of the detained men had the same name as the defendant in the bill sticking offence in Falaise Road.

Hastings came under a new Defence Regulations Act, which made it a twenty-mile deep Defence Area. Nobody was allowed to enter the area except on business and all holidaymakers and day trippers were banned. Arrivals by any form of transport were liable to be stopped and questioned and a demand could be made for identity cards to be produced. Visitors were turned back if they did not have good reason to be in the area. It is hardly surprising that the anxiety about spies and Fifth Columnists intensified. A Hastings woman wrote a letter on the subject to a national newspaper, The Sunday Graphic, saying that there were four German nurses working in a local hospital, not named but thought to be the now demolished Buchanan Hospital. The woman claimed that a German nurse had been seen turning off the radio, when the British National Anthem was playing. (This was not an offence). The whole allegation was denied by the Buchanan Hospital authorities, who said that the services of two of the German nurses had been dispensed with some time previously and the remaining two, one of whom was married to a serving British soldier, were held in high esteem by their colleagues. Rumour and depressing speculation was rife in the town and via Vigilant's column the Regional Officer of Information demanded: "Chatterbugs-Shut Up! Too much defeatist talk is playing the enemy's game". It seems pub clientele were the worst offenders. An Order in Council was made so that anyone found guilty of publishing reports or statements relating to matters of the war likely to cause alarm or despondency could be sentenced to one month's imprisonment, with or without a £50 fine.

In late May, under this climate of fear and suspicion a young man was apprehended on the Firehills by a police constable. The man was described as being of swarthy appearance, respectably dressed and wearing horn-rimmed spectacles. The visitor had come from London and was staying in lodgings in Milward Road. His room was searched and he was later charged with having documents in his possession that contained information that would be useful to the enemy, namely; ordnance survey maps of five different areas, which had rings marked round several places that might be military installations and a notebook that listed a number of addresses, including four in Switzerland. When apprehended, the young man was writing a letter, he claimed it was to his mother. The letter began "Dear Ma" and was said to refer to military matters and such things as signposts, evacuation and the blackout. When charged, the defendant said that he had no intention of helping the enemy. At the end of June 1940 the suspect was again closely questioned in the Hastings Magistrates' Court on each piece of evidence and was also asked to declare if he was a member of the Peace Pledge Union (a pacifist organisation) or a conscientious objector. He denied both suggestions and was able to provide reasonable explanations for his possession of the suspect items. These turned out to be merely a family address book and maps for a walking tour. The defendant was dismissed with a caution but the "evidence" was destroyed.

Feelings on the apparent failure of local young men in Hastings to do their national duty prompted a resident to write to Vigilant: "I sat on the seafront and counted over 100 young men in mufti (civilian clothing) walking by". Vigilant rose to their defence saying that the young men observed had probably already registered for duty but had not yet been called up, unless they are exempted by being Conscientious Objectors, adding, "Fortunately, there are few of these in Hastings." Under the new Defence Regulations, a locally well-known, "casual wayfarer", Everard George Boag, aged 57, was charged with entering a prohibited area. One can only think that the arresting officer, PC Leader was not familiar with Boag, when he spotted him at Warrior Square Station at 3.25am one July morning. At Hastings Police Station, Boag, who described himself as British, could not produce an identity card or proof of residence; he said that he had intended applying for a traveller's card. He had thought that police would vouch for him and help him to get the card. In court, Sub-Inspector Church said that Boag had never been registered; witnesses said that he had been seen around the town on and off for years; he usually carried a sack, containing more sacks, on which he slept in the open. He was remanded in custody for a week. More was learned of Boag at his next court appearance. Born in 1883, he had joined the

Royal Rifles in 1904 and was called to the colours in 1914 and was severely wounded in France. He was demobilized in 1920 and took to the road in 1921, since when he had travelled the country, making his first appearance in Hastings in the 1930s. Mr Boag was a cultured man, being both musical and a linguist and of a good family. A prison sentence of one month was passed and the Clerk of the Court, Colonel F G Langham, said that Mr Boag had committed a serious offence: "This is wartime and your conduct is not good enough". When sentenced, Mr Boag, who had a clean record with no previous convictions protested: "Don't you think you are a little unjust sir?" Ex

George Everard Boag.
Wayfarer and eccentric

Police Constable Kenneth Buddle first encountered Mr Boag post-war: "He loved music and used to sit on the promenade and listen to concerts at the bandstand. There was a cafe on the seafront that used to give Mr Boag a pot of tea every morning and one day he didn't turn up. Somebody went to the St Leonards golf course, where Mr Boag lived in an old hut and they found him laid up with a broken ankle. He was taken to hospital where they nursed him and also trimmed his long hair and unruly beard". Mr Boag continued to be part of local life until his death in 1968. This seemed to be an unfortunate period for vagrants: Shortly after Boag's arrest it was the turn of an aged female tramp to appear in court. She wept in the dock when she was sentenced to 14 days in prison for having no identity card, which she said she had lost two months previously. She told the bench she had been travelling for several days on foot from Cranbrook, to get to relatives in Mayfield. She had been a vagrant for eight years, since her husband died.

Vigilant's reference to the "few" conscientious objectors in the town may have prompted the response from NALGO, (National Association of Local Government Officers) voiced at a Town Council meeting, during which they deplored the continuing employment of COs by the Corporation and asked the council to terminate that employment forthwith. The Town Clerk said that there were only two employees, aged 21 and 22, who held such opinions, adding, "Which the law permits; the government has passed an Act that gives these people the right to object." However after two minutes discussion the council moved that both young men should be interviewed and sacked. Not every case of conscientious objection was treated with this kind of summary justice. A local builder applied to the South Eastern Tribunal to register as a conscientious objector. He had already joined the Auxiliary Fire Service, in a part-time capacity, because the AFS was dedicated to saving life and property, for which he was qualified and this was in accordance with his principles as a preacher with the Religious Brethren. His beliefs prevented him from entering the armed forces but he felt if people saw him in uniform they would think he had joined up. The tribunal decreed that the man could register as a CO, providing he remained in the AFS or took up ambulance or agricultural work.

After the appalling slaughter during WWI it is a wonder that there was any urge to volunteer for military service in WWII. There was some pressure from society for men to join up in WWII but almost none of the hysterical patriotism that was seen during the early stages of The Great War, when women handed out white feathers to men who did not volunteer for military service. Those who willingly came forward in WWII were probably inspired by a variety of motives: There were those who understood the threat of Nazism and wanted to destroy it; others imagined service life would be an adventure. The opportunists thought that early entry into the services would make it easier to get 'safe' or prestigious positions. Many who were unemployed or in dull jobs or marriages embraced enlisting as an escape from their circumstances.

On 27th April 1939, Parliament passed the Military Training Act. This act introduced conscription for men aged 20 and 21, who were required to undertake six months' military training. As war was declared, the government passed the National Service (Armed Forces) Act, which made all men between 18 and 41 liable for conscription. The registration of all men in each age group in turn began on 21st October 1939, commencing with those aged 20 to 23. By May 1940, registration had extended only as far as men aged 27. On 18th

December 1941, the National Service Act was passed by Parliament, which would eventually oblige all those eligible to participate in war work of some kind.

In WWI, conscientious objectors had suffered public abuse, persecution and sometimes extremely cruel treatment while in custody but by 1939 attitudes had changed and there was a tendency for most authorities to show some tolerance in dealing with them. In the interval between the wars many pacifists had found respected places in society; in religious life, politics, the arts and other fields. This led churchmen and other public figures to denounce victimization of conscientious objectors. Even Winston Churchill publicly spoke out against persecution of COs as, 'odious to the British people'. This tolerance deprived the cause of martyrs and appeared to weaken the pacifism movement rather than strength it. The local tribunals before which COs appeared during WWII were different from those of WWI. The new tribunals had five members; one of whom was approved by the Trades Unions and none from the War Office. The objector had the right of appeal to a higher tribunal. The tribunals varied greatly in their attitudes towards conscientious objection to military service and the proportions totally rejected for exemption ranged from 6 per cent to 41 per cent. The political and moral views of the tribunal chairman were vitally important. It was very difficult to get a fair hearing in London, especially during the Blitz. There were 52,000 conscientious objectors in WWII. Nearly half these were allowed to register as COs but only on the condition that they took up approved work or stayed in their current jobs. Some 15,000 registered for non-combatant duties in the armed forces and over 12,000 were refused registration and remained liable to call up. Many COs were sent to work in the coal mines, creating the anomaly of miners who wanted to enlist in the military services but could not because they were in essential labour and reluctant miners, who found themselves in the job because they did not want to serve.

As the phoney war ended, with the start of the bombing of civilians in the summer of 1940, attitudes towards COs hardened. Some private employers sacked pacifists and 119 local authorities dismissed them or suspended their employment for the duration of the war. About 5000 male and 500 female objectors were sent to prison; over 1000 appeared before a court martial and were imprisoned in military jails. There were over 500 cases of men and 90 of women who refused to perform fire-watching duties; they received short prison sentences as did those who refused to take up conscripted industrial work. A special non-combatant corp in the army, founded in the spring of 1940, had almost 7,000 members. Conscientious objectors in the parachute field ambulances were among the first to land in Europe on D-Day and were also numbered among bomb-disposal squads.

After the first air raid in July 1940, Vigilant weighed in with words of encouragement and advice, urging the townspeople to remain calm but not to become complacent about the possibility of a German invasion. From mid-July, a 10.00pm to 5.00am curfew was put into operation on the Hastings and St Leonards seafront. The first person to break the curfew was a 61 year old woman, an alcoholic, well known to the police, who was found, drunk and incapable at 10.45 pm near the Lifeboat Station at East Parade. She was fined one pound for each offence. Even police officers were not exempt from the curfew; two out-of-uniform constables, discovered in the banned area, were fined £1 each-with time to pay. Deputy Police Chief Buddle said that there could be no discrimination in the courts and even a police officer, unless on duty, was not allowed in the banned area after curfew. Generally, as far as court reports reveal, curfew breakers seemed to be mostly lovers or drunks! A legal procedure of a more pleasant nature was affected by war: Sirens sounded during a wedding ceremony at St John's Church Upper St Leonards in September, when the Rural Dean was officiating at the marriage of 17 year-old Elsie Ball and William Coussens. The ceremony was resumed in a shelter under the church, with the organist accompanying the service on the piano installed in the shelter.

In September 1940, a Hastings woman, who had been on a destruction spree was arrested for being drunk and disorderly. Whilst under the influence, she had sawn through a wood and barbed wire barrier, because she objected to it being near her Kent Cottages home, in All Saints' Street. After her arrest she smashed a window in The Central Police Station charge room, sustaining injuries that necessitated a trip to the Royal East Sussex Hospital for treatment. She said she smashed the window because a constable had looked through it and said, "Poor

Little Bessie." She was sentenced to three months in prison and one month's hard labour, to run consecutively and to pay the cost of damages or serve a further 14 days. When he was asked about, "Little Bessie", Ex-Inspector Banks said that he remembered her well as something of a nuisance. "She used to go about with a little wooden handcart and she carried a stick with a brass knob on its end. She was very aggressive and when she was drunk she used to hit people and break shop windows with the stick; she also used it to kill the street pigeons and take them home to cook and eat. She was frequently arrested. It was the custom of the station sergeant to check on prisoners every hour, via a hatch in the cell door. On one occasion Bessie was waiting for the appearance of Police Sergeant Dann and as he looked through the hatch she punched him on the nose". Ex-Inspector Thompson recalled her as: "A woman of medium height with a stocky build. She could fight like a man; on one occasion I saw her have a stand up fist fight with a man. She would write scurrilous slogans in public places about local people; one in particular made vulgar and humorous reference to a supposed homosexual liaison between a local man and a vicar!" Even among the sober citizens of the town there was a feeling of resentment when their path was barred due to wartime emergencies. They had accepted that the beach and pier were closed to public access but according to Vigilant they were challenging the police,

when they found that their customary right of way was cut off by a rope or barrier, after a bombing raid. A 38 year-old working jeweller was stopped by the police and could not produce his identity card and he failed to produce the card within 24 hours at Hastings Police Station. He then refused to complete an identity card registration form other than with his name, saying that if he added his occupation he would put it as, "The dangerous one of trying to live as a Christian in a pagan civilization". The prosecuting solicitor, Mr. McCall, said that the possession of an identity card was of the greatest importance in times of crisis and this was the most definitive case of defying the law he had encountered. The jeweller was fined £5 and sentenced to one month in prison.

The compulsory identity card was part of the 1939 National Registration Act, under which a National Register was compiled, containing details of all citizens. National identity cards were then issued to all civilians. The cards bore details of name, address, gender, age, marital status, occupation, profession, trade or employment and stated if the card owner was a member of the Military or Auxiliary Forces or Civil Defence Services. The reasons for the identity card scheme were the expected major dislocation of the population, caused by mobilization and mass evacuation and the wartime need for

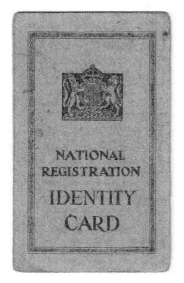

complete manpower control, in order to maximize the efficiency of the war economy. A further reason was the likelihood of rationing. It was felt that the imminence of rationing demanded an up-to-date system of standardized registration, so that controls could be introduced as easily as possible.

The compilation of the register was entrusted to enumerators who were responsible for collecting the data. All civilians were legally obliged to carry the card and produce it on demand to a constable in uniform, any other authorised person or to produce it at a court hearing within 24 hours. In September 1939, vital freedoms of the individual had been ended over a period of a few days, with hardly any debate. In addition, the Government was given the power to ban meetings that it felt might create public disorder, cause an offence or be, "prejudicial to the defence of the realm". It gave enormously wide and general powers to the police and, indeed, to any person authorised, to the delight of some petty officials and wartime volunteers. These powers extended to the Home Guard, who aggravated the general public, by setting up road blocks and demanding to see the identity cards of travellers, even if they had been known to them all their lives! Offences under the National Registration Act included giving false information, impersonation, forgery of an identity card, and unauthorized disclosure of information. For these offences, maximum penalties on summary conviction were a £50 fine and/or three months in prison, and on conviction on indictment a £100 fine and/or two years in prison. It was also an offence to fail to comply with any other requirement under the Act and the maximum penalty was a £5 fine or one month in prison or both. The Act applied to the whole of the United Kingdom and was to remain in force until 22nd May 1952. No separate statistics of offences under the National Registration Act are available for the years 1939-45, since they are recorded under `other misdemeanors'.

For safety reasons the ARP issued an order that no perambulators, dogs or smoking would be allowed in public air raid shelters. A householder in St Helen's Road was commending for putting a notice in their window to invite in any passers by who were caught in an air raid, to share the family's shelter. As the war progressed this became quite a common practice. Pat Jones, of Hastings, aged 93, backed this up by saying that if she was at home when a raid started she would look out in the street to ask anybody who was walking along her road to come inside and shelter. She said that she remembered being out in the town in an air raid and seeing a German plane fly in very low, level with the sea and then rise up over the pier and then above the cliffs, on a tip and run raid. Sometimes the pilots machine-gunned people who were out in the streets. In these circumstances, if there was no shelter nearby, people would just lie down on the pavement or in the gutter.

Vigilant had not finished with the subject of air raid sirens. His next complaint was that they went on for too long, interfering with the work of the Observer Corp, who were listening for the sound of approaching enemy aircraft and also discouraging people from hastening to the shelters. Although by September 1940 the Hastings population had suffered fatalities in bombing raids, blackout regulation offenders (both the willful and the careless, as Vigilant described them) still appeared in court and were fined.

Looting in WWII was officially punishable with death, by hanging or shooting, but no such sentence was ever passed for the crime. It was not only bombed houses that received the looters' attentions. Many families had been obliged to abandon their dwellings under evacuation schemes and in some towns an entire street was stripped of its residents' goods and chattels by looters. So bold did the gangs of looters become that they would carry out their work during air raids, when the police were occupied elsewhere and the noise and confusion masked their activities. Looted goods were not covered under the provisions of the War Damage Act, so the victims of the looting from their bombed houses suffered a double blow, as they were not only homeless but bereft of their possessions.

A number of British and German planes crashed in the Hastings area and if young boys reached the crash site before the authorities, they took full advantage of the chance to loot the plane of whatever they could find; this often included live ammunition and armaments. Ivor White now aged 78 recalls when a Heinkel 111 crashed near his Battle home, "The field where the twin-engine bomber had crashed was littered with debris and I soon found some aluminum tubing, which I later made into decorative finger-rings and cigarette lighters. My salvage collection included many panel instruments from aircraft, ammunition, and two complete 20mm cannons. All of the ammunition was rendered harmless by extracting the bullet and emptying the cordite from the cartridges. The detonator caps were then exploded, while held in a vice, using a hammer and a nail, before re-assembling and polishing the complete items for display. I had no fear of guns and explosives in those days as I had been using a 12-bore shotgun since I was big enough to hold one to my shoulder. When my brother and I took the 20mm cannons we decided to hide them in the attic of our house; they might have still been in the attic until this day, had it not been for the local policeman, PC Barrow, who lived next door but one, telling my Mum that the authorities were looking for people who had visited the crash scene. This was probably a friendly warning to the effect that if her boys had removed anything they should get rid of it. Policemen often did that kind of thing then. Living and working in the community gave them a very pastoral attitude to the local people, especially the children. So we dumped our findings in a woodland pond, where they may still be today. If anyone ever finds them, it will give them something to think about!"

Petty looting from bombed houses was also perpetrated by young and teenaged boys but it was a more serious example of this offence, with a bizarre twist, which was heard in Hastings Police Court in October 1940. Two young men, aged 16 and 20, borrowed an idea from the exploits of a character made famous in books and films and left notes signed, "The Saint", after stealing 5/3d (27p) from a gas meter in the ruins of a bombed house. They were among the first to be prosecuted in Hastings under the new legislation on looting. They also stole from the property a 45 calibre service revolver, a German made automatic pistol and several rounds of rifle and pistol ammunition. At the scene they left a number of pencilled notes, one of which said, "Tell the local constable to wait a while, as we are enjoying a Churchman's Number One; signed, The Saint." (The reference is to the cigarette; Churchman's Number One and is a paraphrasing of a well known advertisement of the day). Detective Sergeant Pike told the court that when he interviewed the older offender he had in his possession an envelope containing building society pass books and a ration book; the envelope was addressed; "To the Flat-Feet-return to owners." It was learned at a subsequent court hearing that the twenty year-old was a major's son and an absentee from the army, in which he had shown exemplary conduct. He was handed over to the military authorities for their jurisdiction. The younger offender was said to be addicted to funfairs; (funfair was the contemporary word for an amusement arcade.) He was sentenced to be detained, to await placement an approved school for three years. The 16 year old appealed against his sentence and Detective Sergeant Pike said, at a later appearance in court, "The defendant has stayed in a voluntary hostel for three months and his conduct has been exemplary." The hostel warden testified to the boy's intelligence and said he had been a healthy influence on others. It was judged that his offence had been a mistaken idea of adventure and his sentence was reduced to two years on probation. Of the soldier in the case nothing more was published. Bearing in mind the soldier's tendency to find nicknames for comrades, it does not need much imagination to think of the one that dogged the offender throughout his service life!

The Detective Sergeant Pike, mentioned in the previous case seems to have been something of a character. He was stocky, red-faced and recalled by Ex-Inspector Thompson as: "A bulldog of a man! He made some excellent captures during his career but was somewhat accident prone when driving. He had one dramatic crash at the double bend near the Langham Pub that caused the spot to be referred to thereafter as Pike's Corner, but not within his hearing!"

Today's Neighbourhood Watch Scheme compares poorly with the close observation that some individuals kept on their community in wartime; these alert citizens were often instrumental in bringing people to court, as in the case of the jobbing gardener with a passion for photography. The offender, a man aged 67, was seen acting in a suspicious manner and trying to hide something under his coat. The witness, a retired man of 68, discerning it was a camera, informed the police. The camera was produced in court with a number of photographic prints, two of bombed, unnamed but important buildings. The defendant said that he had been interested in photography for nine years and had photographed various houses before the war and wanted a set of contrasting pictures. The police found other films at the defendant's home, plus a printed extract from a War Office list that stated what objects could and could not be photographed. The offender was sentenced to six weeks in prison and a fine of £10 was imposed for photographing bombed buildings without a written permit. Superintendent Buddle said that the police took a very serious view of such offences and commended the witness as a good example to others. Vigilant took up the national security theme by admonishing vicars, warning them to be more discreet in their parish magazines: "I am not suggesting there are Fifth Columnists in the clergy but they should be as scrupulous as the press and avoid mentioning such matters as bombs falling close to the church. These small details can add to the enemy's information jig-saw, to which the Minister of Air and Home Security referred in his recent broadcast."

The start of the blackout in 1939 had brought restrictions to the power of car headlights, which were henceforth to be concealed behind a louvred metal cover; the three louvres were about three inches long and half an inch wide and deflected the light downwards. New lighting restrictions for motor vehicles came into force on October 23rd 1940, which stated that the aperture for side, rear and stop lights must not exceed one inch in diameter and be visible at 30 yards but not at 300 yards. Prior to the law coming into force there was a three-week press and radio campaign and a police, after-dark checking and advice campaign. In spite of this, November 1940 found six offenders before the court under the new Defence of the Realm Act. After a long deliberation by the magistrates they decided to be lenient as these were first offenders and they handed down fines of only 10/-(50p), £1 and £2 for what were serious breaches of the law. There were also new regulations introduced concerning the shielding of hand torches, already screened by two thicknesses of tissue paper. A defendant before the court said that he did not know of the new regulations in reference to the use of an unscreened torch and the Clerk of the Court admitted: "I am afraid that I am in the same state of ignorance as you". A fine of 5/-(25p) was imposed on the hapless offender.

Frederick Goodsell – "Vigilant"

From time to time, Vigilant posed moral dilemmas to his readers: In one example he wrote: "Should Hastings Lifeboat rescue Nazis?" Councillor A R Wilson, a volunteer with Hastings Lifeboat and a former seaman, who had served in WWI, wrote to the Hastings and St Leonards Observer, saying that he wished to clear up any misunderstanding: "The brutality of the Nazis in machine gunning those attempting to rescue their fellow countrymen was a despicable action but the lifeboat would still go to rescue German airmen, but unwillingly." In late November 1940, The Hastings and St Leonards Observer had a new editor. It was Frederick Goodsell, the former assistant editor, who was almost certainly Vigilant. He was young for the post, being under forty. A former Hastings Grammar School boy, Goodsell had joined the newspaper as a cub reporter in 1926. He marked his promotion with an attack in his Flotsam and Jetsam column on the offence of looting: "This is a serious crime and magistrates have issued a warning that those brought before the bench for this offence will be punished severely. It is certainly going on and all decent people hope that the offenders will be caught and punished. Collecting fragments from a crashed enemy plane is also against Public Security Regulations, as the parts could reveal important technical devices to the experts." He also referred to scrounging from bombed premises and reminded citizens that no person, except the police, the military or the ARP has a right to remove anything from a bomb-damaged building. Vigilant reported that the looting from scrap metal dumps had ceased, probably because the all valuable items had been stolen. He went on to deplore the outbreak of looting from the pig-bins, put outside residences for what little waste food there was, to be collected for fattening pigs. A local pig keeper wrote to Vigilant, defending those who helped themselves from pig-bins, saying that as the town's hotels were no longer in business, waste food was in short supply. Vigilant responded via his column, pointing out that the bins belonged to the Women's Royal Voluntary Service, who sold the collected waste to the corporation; therefore it was theft if permission to take it was not obtained from the householder.

Infringements of the rationing regulations continued to be a regular subject of magistrates' court cases: A Battle grocer was prosecuted by the Food Control Committee for supplying the mother of a delicate son with an extra 2 ounces of butter and 4 ounces of margarine, above her proper ration. The grocer claimed they were rations surplus to his own family's needs. His management of the ration system underwent a thorough investigation and it was concluded that he had infringed Regulation 40 of the Food Acts and that he and the customer should be made an example of, "lest the whole structure of rationing should fall to the ground." The customer was fined 21/- (£1.05) with 10/6 (55p) costs and the grocer £17. 12. 00 (£17.60p). The slipping of a little extra rationed food to the needy or to favoured customers was very commonplace and several people interviewed referred to it happening to them.

As a wartime informality, Judge F. K. Archer, KC, took to sitting in Hastings County Court without his wig and robes, which he said in no way detracted from the businesslike dignity of the court. The judge said: "Counsel who appears unrobed before a judge is bound by legal etiquette to apologise for this. It is a tradition that a barrister, unclad in wig and gown may be seen in court but cannot be heard unless he has adequate reasons for appearing unrobed. These days there are plenty of good reasons."

The police administration duties of Ex-Inspector Banks brought him into frequent contact with local solicitors. He spoke of Mr S Penry-Davey: "He was a very well known Hastings solicitor during the war. He ran an extensive practice from 23, Cambridge Road. (The rear of the Victorian property that is currently being re-built as a media centre). When he was acting for the defence, his cross examinations of the police and civilian witnesses were very searching and he frequently won arguments with opposition lawyers and barristers. His son, a brilliant scholar, attended Hastings Grammar School and while waiting to go to university he became an assistant teacher at Summerfields School for Boys. Penry-Davy Junior excelled at university and law school; he became an outstanding solicitor and was appointed a judge on one of the northern circuits". Bringing the story up to date, Ex-Inspector Banks continued: "Judge Penry-Davey was one of the three judges who dealt with the first appeal of Sion Jenkins, the Deputy Head Master of Hastings Grammar School, who was convicted of murdering his foster-daughter in Hastings' Lower Park Road

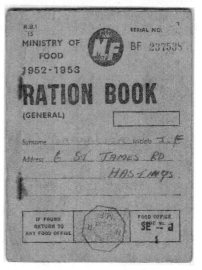

in 1998. Jenkins made a second appeal on the grounds that Judge Mr Penry-Davy was biased because he had been a pupil at Hastings Grammar School many years previously. The Appeal Court dismissed this appeal, ruling that the judge's place of education was irrelevant.

The matter of the pig-bin looting eventually appeared in court, as Hastings' first case heard under the October 1941 Salvage of Waste Order. The defendant was accused of taking waste food without the consent of the owners, namely vegetable and potato peelings, placed in a bin outside a house for official collectors. When approached by the police the defendant said: "If I don't feed my pigs I shall be pinched for cruelty for starving them." He said that he had offered the corporation the same price for the waste food that his competitor was paying but his offer was refused. He thought that was unfair, as the other pig-keeper was an outsider from the town and not a ratepayer but was getting an advantage at the expense of ratepayers. The pig-bin looter was fined 10/- (50p).

Vigilant said that he always found it interesting to read the Hastings Chief Constable's annual report on licensing and it was more so for the year ending 31st December 1940. There had been only 25 summonses for drunkenness, 10 females and 15 males; 10 of the offenders were not local and the female convictions were the lowest for years. The nearest approach to these figures was in 1936, when there was a total of 40 convictions. The highest year for convictions for drunkenness was in 1926 when there were 73. The Chief Constable, Mr Bell, said two of the reasons for the low figure for 1940 were that so many people had left Hastings and no summer holiday visitors had arrived. He commended the licensees in Hastings and St Leonards: "Many surprise visits have been made by the police to various public houses and they were found to be well conducted, with no excessive drinking."

As if to confound this report, "Dear Little Bessie" appeared in court again, in mid-January. It was stated that she had thrown a whisky glass in the face of the licensee of the Rising Sun, who was present in court and wearing dark glasses. The prosecuting solicitor, Mr. Harold Glenister, said that the defendant threw the glass in a fit of temper. Three soldiers entered the pub and when Bessie's dog approached them she called it away saying, "Come away from those ****** thieves; all soldiers are thieves!" When told by the licensee not to talk like that she resorted to obscene language and threw the glass at him, which broke. (The broken glass was produced in court). Bessie denied throwing the glass at the licensee but said it was aimed at an organ, which she claimed was hers, in the bar. Superintendent Buddle said that the defendant had many convictions since coming to Hastings in 1924, including 8 assaults on the police and private persons. In this case she was fined £5 with 15/- (75p) costs. There followed an altercation with the Clerk of the Court when she was asked if she wanted time to pay, she responded with, "Yes, a twelvemonth." "Ridiculous", said the Chairman of the bench, pointing out that the alternative was two months in prison. Bessie said she would appeal and tore up her fines payment card in court.

Hastings has a long history of smuggling; in the distant past the usual illicit commodities were brandy, tobacco, tea and lace but it was contraband of a very different nature that brought a case before the court in the spring of 1941. Adding a touch of style to the charge was the fact the defendant was a titled lady. It was stated that she had written letters to Ireland; to her daughter-in-law, a friend and a gardener, asking them to post food to her. The letter was intercepted by the censor and handed to the Divisional Food Officer. The lady was charged with attempting to smuggle goods into this country, namely; four pounds of sugar and three quarters of a pound of butter. She claimed ignorance of the law but was fined £5.00 with £1.16.00 (£1.80p) costs. Had she but known it, Her Ladyship had no need to go so far afield for her illegal supplies. In the same month, a grocer in Hastings' All Saints Street was fined for disposing of a large quantity of surplus rations, outside the rationing system. He said that the problem of excess rationed foodstuffs, butter, sugar and margarine, was caused by some of his customers in the Old Town being too poor to buy the quantities to which they were entitled. Food shops owners in Hastings were having a very hard time; they had lost a major source of business when the war caused the closure of hotels and guest houses and the mass evacuation of the population had led to a further loss of income. Many small traders found themselves in Hastings County Court, because of debts. Judge F K Archer praised Hastings' hard-hit tradesmen during a court hearing of a debt claim. The judge said that what impressed him was their honesty and pluck. "Most of them do not say 'My business is ruined by the war, I cannot pay anything,' they take on some other job and re-pay every last farthing. We cannot go hitting them when they are down."

Hastings Town Council turned its attention to the question of singing in air raid shelters, with particular reference to Hastings Caves. Not only singing but smoking and the playing of instruments had been banned in air raid shelters by the Ministry of Local Security. The Town Council was also concerned that local residents might be starting to regard the caves as a type of Hastings Corporation dwelling and it was suggested that living there might give people an excuse to not pay rent and rates. Councillor S. Riddle thought that the rules against singing and music, which kept up peoples' spirits, were "piffle" and as for the caves being regarded as a permanent home, people were only there because they were obliged to be. One of these nighttime cave dwellers was Kathleen Vaughan, aged 98, who said that they took their own mattresses and food into the caves every night but a hot drink was provided by the shelter wardens in the mornings.

Cave dwellers settle down for the night under the stern eye of a police officer

Arrest for breaking the law with reference to the defence area regulations became commonplace and it demonstrated the alertness of the police and other emergency services but almost none of the offenders had malicious intent and the court sometimes revealed unexpected compassion in judgment. A grieving widower, whose wife was killed in a major bombing incident in Queen's Road, Hastings on October 5th 1940, was in court for entering a prohibited zone and being in the same after the curfew. He had come back to the town to visit his wife's grave. When she was killed he was working in London and the first he knew of his wife's death was when he was stopped in the street by a Home Guard Corporal, who conveyed the terrible news. Since then the defendant's behaviour had been strange. He was advised, by Acting Clerk, Mr. Raymond Goldsack, to plead not guilty to the first charge of entering a defence zone and the charge was withdrawn. The defendant apologized for the curfew offence and said that he knew nothing about the law. The case was dismissed on the payment of 10/- (50p) costs. Mr Raymond Goldsack was a close friend of Ex-Inspector Banks and he recalled that in the course of his work he was often obliged to visit the Acting Clerk's office in Middle Street. He used to find Mr Goldsack's son there, who was a pupil at Hastings Grammar School, closely studying the numerous volumes of law and discussing complex legal issues with his father. Raymond gave the boy every encouragement, as he wished to qualify as a solicitor. The boy eventually became a brilliant lawyer and was appointed a judge.

Vigilant turned his attention to the wartime public transport system in Hasting and St Leonards and the government demand that housewives should complete their journeys by bus before 4.00pm and leave public transport available for home-going workers. Vigilant noticed that a bus, on which he was going home after work, was: "Full of leisured and leisurely ladies, who insisted that the conductor stopped the bus for them at the end of their road". There were many who could not afford the modest luxury of public transport: Doris Dann aged 91, said that she walked wherever she needed to go, with her children in the pram, and thought nothing of walking up to six miles or more to visit her mother.

A case of systematic looting that came before the court in 1941 was

that of a 20 year-old man who had gained illegal entry to his aunt's house after she had been evacuated from Hastings. He set about removing her belongings and sold them to a second hand dealer in the town, who had also been entering abandoned properties on his own account and stealing goods in large quantities. On the proceeds of the sale of these goods the 34 year-old dealer was living a riotous life and drinking heavily. The police were helped with their investigations by a burgled householder, who was able to identify a laundry mark on linen goods, found in the second hand shop. The dealer was sentenced to 12 months' hard labour, while the younger man, said to be of low mentality and with previous convictions, was given three months hard labour. (The sentence of hard labour tended to be of shorter duration than that of penal servitude. Hard labour was usually carried out within the prison and took the form of hand sewing coarse, canvas mailbags or some other rough or heavy hand work. Penal servitude was most

Sewing mail bags in prison

often undertaken by gangs of prisoners, outside the prison and was arduous work like rock breaking or road building, under the eyes of armed guards). Elaine Wiltshire contributed this anecdote on looting from the wartime memories of her mother Mrs. Burkin, who reveals that even the most trifling items were not safe from looters. Elaine was born in March 1937 and her father was a jobbing gardener/handyman. At the outbreak of war, one of his employers decided to leave her Bexhill home and take her four children to a safer area. She asked Mrs. Burkin to keep an eye on her house and garage, where she had locked the household china and her children's books. Little Elaine was fond of books and her mother would sometimes borrow from the collection in the garage. Mrs. Burkin wrote: "Elaine and I sometimes used to borrow a book from the boxes in the garage. One Sunday afternoon I got there and I found that the door had been forced and a lot of the books and china were missing. I called at the police station to report the loss and to give a description of the missing articles, as best as I could remember. Nothing more was heard until my husband, Harry, came home on leave and we were walking round one afternoon and we saw a table outside a second hand shop with books on it; some of them had the names of the children of my husband's employer written inside. So Harry phoned the police, who were most casual and said that many books come off the press and my husband said: "But not with the name of the rightful owner written inside them". The police were soon at the second hand shop and they found china and books from the garage. They also went to the shopkeeper's home and it was an Aladdin's Cave of things from other burglaries. I had to attend court to give evidence, which was quite an experience. When it was all over the articles were to be returned to the lady who owned them but she said we might as well have them, as we had been put to so much trouble".

Italy's declaration of the war against Britain in 1941 added to the source of suspected secret agents and few new arrivals escaped the notice of neighbours. A British born woman, with Italian parents and married to an Italian, moved to Hastings with her family after having been bombed out in London. She was arrested in Hastings, as it was discovered she had broken the conditions that prevented her, as a registered alien, from travelling for more than 5 miles from her home and as a further offence, she had not informed the police of her arrival in Hastings. In her defence the Clerk to the Court said her husband must be a respected person, as he had not been interned and was working in London. The woman apologized for the trouble she had caused and was given a conviction but no penalty.

During a Town Council meeting, the Watch Committee praised the police for the decrease in Hastings crime figures, as revealed in the 1941 annual report of the Chief Constable, Mr J Bell. There was a fall in the number of crimes from 544 to 450. Among the crimes listed were 15 cases of looting and 61 motoring offences. There was, however an increase in juvenile crime, blamed on the continuing closure of school. A total of 125 boys had been placed with the male officer, Mr. P T Hogan, who stated that for years certain children had lacked parental control and that due to the war, family life was upset for many more. Vigilant, uncharacteristically, spoke up in defence of a particular kind of juvenile offender: "What must be considered is that the youngster who gets into mischief and figures in wild escapades is often of the type from which fighter pilots and daring seamen are made; the raw material of a desperado is not so different from that of a war medal winner". Of local girls he was less approving, noting that the war has brought restlessness among young girls of an unstable type, due to the proximity of military service units. "Moral welfare workers are finding these factors are already making themselves felt."

In July 1941, the Police Matron, Mrs. Alice Paine, retired from the position she had held since 1915. Supt Buddle said that Mrs. Paine had never been known to complain, even when she had to turn out in the middle of the night or was asked to escort hardened criminals and murderers into custody. The prisoners always had a good word for her and in turn, Mrs. Paine said she had felt very sorry for some. She had saved two prisoners from committing suicide. The departing matron was presented with a gold silk eiderdown and bedspread, as an appreciation of her 26 years' service. A newspaper photograph of the presentation, which took place in the Queens Road courtroom, shows in the background the oak clad walls, decorative shields and the magisterial bench; the view that was seen by the unfortunates in the

The interior of Hastings Magistrates' Court 1941

dock. After Mrs Alice Paine retired, her position was taken by Mrs Goodsell, who was the wife of the town hall caretaker. The couple lived in a house in Station Road, (now demolished) near the police station, thus putting Mrs Goodsell conveniently available to search any female prisoners who were brought in.

Chief Constable Bell left Hastings Police Force in 1941; he accepted the post of Assistant Chief Constable in Manchester. He had taken up his post in Hastings in 1933, aged 34. He was an authority on the police box and became responsible for reorganizing police work locally. Between 1929 and 1930 a considerable number of police boxes were built in the borough and in conjunction with these, a revised beat system was introduced in 1930. Up until then, beats still had to be

Mr. Joseph Bell, Chief Constable of Hastings from 1933 to 1942

worked on prescribed routes and to a strict timetable. Under this system of patrolling it was possible for criminals to log accurately the times at which a constable would be in a particular area. This method of working also discouraged the initiative of men working the patrols. In June 1935, a new system of policing came into operation, involving a redistribution of strength and the reorganization of the beats with discretionary working. Chief Constable Joseph Bell was the ARP Controller of the borough and established the Special Constabulary as a uniformed auxiliary force. Superintendent William Buddle was appointed Acting Chief of Police on Bell's Departure.

Yet another example of the complexity of the rationing system brought the St Leonards branch of The Retail Cooperative Society to court, after a case of confusion regarding the substitution of one type of rationed fat for another. The Ministry of Food regulations stated, "You may purchase margarine instead of cooking fat but you may not have more than your ration of cooking fat (2ounces), even if you have less than your ration of margarine". No wonder errors were made by shop assistants and they became easy prey to the ever-present and secret "food police." Substitution of another kind occurred when the manager of the local branch of grocers, The India Tea Company, supplied the matron of a nursing home with a joint of smoked bacon but invoiced it as cake, which was not rationed. This came to light when the food enforcer discovered the paper-wrapped parcel, as it was about to be delivered. In both cases fines were handed down to shop staff as well as the company.

Vigilant commented in August on the increasing cases of pilfering from vegetable gardens and allotments. A local gardener told him: "I don't mind if the people who steal the vegetables eat them but when they rob your plot to sell them, you feel really sore!" Vigilant hoped that no more would be heard of this crime, unless it was from a police court. Within weeks, two cases of crop stealing appeared in court but their nature was so pathetic that they seem more likely to invoke pity than condemnation. The gardener at a house in Hollington Lane saw a woman in the orchard with her arms full of apples, valued at 1/- (5p). She pleaded with the gardener not to report her and said she had never done anything like it before. In court she first claimed that she did not know it was an orchard and then went on to say a boy gave her the apples. Acting Chief Buddle said that there had been numerous complaints about stealing from orchards and allotments; the woman was fined 10/- (50p). In October an elderly widow, with a brain

I was front-page news
a year ago . . . more precious
than gold to those lucky enough to get a pound of me. That was because you relied on having me brought to you from abroad. Yet, if women and older children, as well as men, are sensible enough to Dig for Victory *NOW*, you can have me ALL THE YEAR ROUND for only the cost of a packet of seeds . . .

YOU SEE, I AM ONE OF THOSE CROPS YOU CAN STORE

DIG FOR VICTORY NOW!

damaged adult son to support, was fined 10/- (50p) for stealing one onion and a handful of runner beans from the crops in a fellow allotment holder's patch. Buddle said, "Over the past 18 months police have had many complaints about thefts from gardens and allotments. In some cases whole rows of vegetables have been cleared. It may seem trivial to bring a case over one onion but it is a very serious matter." The onion theft highlighted a national problem with this particular vegetable. There was an acute shortage of onion seed in the early 1940s. Pre-war Britain had relied on the importation of onion and many kinds other of vegetable seeds. So before home produced seed

WWII prison conditions

could be gathered and sown, onions particularly were in very short supply and therefore precious. It was said that in a raffle one onion raised £4.3.00 (£4.14).

In mid-August, a conscientious objector, aged 24, appeared in Hastings Police Court and was sentenced to six months in prison. He had refused to submit to a military service medical examination, an offence for which he had already been fined. He had registered as a CO but his name had been removed from the list. He had offered to do work on the land or with the ARP but said that he would not participate in, "the present madness." He was sentenced to six months in prison and the Chairman of the Bench announced: "It does not follow that because this is the first case of its kind we have had that the sentence will be the same in future." A subsequent offender, who said that he answered to a Higher Authority, was charged with repeated refusals to take a military medical on religious grounds; he was given a fine of £2.00 and six months in prison. Vigilant told his readers that the purveyors of the Peace News had been fixing copies of the publication on some people's house gates and doors. He found a copy "decorating or desecrating" his own property. This pacifist magazine asked residents to complain to their MP, Mr. Hely-Hutchinson, about the imprisonment of conscientious objectors. Vigilant wrote: "I find it difficult to understand the mentality of these people, who insult us with this publication or why the government permits it to be printed."

The serious question of beer shortage was raised at the August meeting of the Licensed Victuallers' Association and a letter from the National Trade Defence Association was read out; it urged licensees to keep their pubs open at weekends, even if it meant closing for one or two evenings during the week. Even with the shortage of beer, a soldier on leave managed to get himself so inebriated that he caused a fracas on a Hastings bus. He and his large brown dog boarded the bus at the town centre at 2.45pm and the soldier started to create a disturbance. When asked by a fellow passenger to be quiet the soldier thrust his fist under the man's nose and then picked a fight with another passenger, who put the soldier off the bus, which he immediately re-boarded and a fight ensued, during which the soldier sustained ear injuries. At his appearance in Hastings Police Court, the soldier was fined £1 for disorderly conduct and £2 for assault. Generally, magistrates tended to deal leniently with soldiers on leave who misbehaved, possibly thinking that further punishment awaited them on their return to barracks, so the sentence in this case was quite heavy.

On Sunday 14th September 1941, a crime of a most horrific nature, involving a soldier and a member of the public, was uncovered in the

Hastings underground car park

underground car park at Hastings Seafront. The car park, opened in June 1936, was part of a major promenade development scheme. The underground structure runs from the White Rock Theatre to Carlisle Parade, near the Town Centre. The area is divided into open-sided bays, each to accommodate one vehicle. During the war, the car park had thick concrete walls installed across its width at 60 feet intervals and the construction was re-deployed as a public air raid shelter, for military accommodation and as a command centre for emergency services and a storage and distribution facility. Viewed in the 21st century, the car park presents an uninviting prospect; its proximity to the sea and the leakage of rain has caused deterioration. In 1941 it was still considered to be one of Hastings modern wonders and a source of pride.

At 6.05 am on the 14th September, a man who was walking through the car park noticed a long stream of blood running from a First Aid Post, which he knew to be the sleeping place of a 74 year-old woman,

Miss J, a retired dressmaker, who had been bombed out in an air raid on Hastings in October 1940; she had been sleeping in the car park ever since. He then saw Miss J's half naked body, lying on a deck chair. He had last heard her alive at 10.45 the previous night, when she was muttering to herself, as she often did. Later in the day the body of a young soldier was found in another part of the car park; he had shot himself. He was 23 year-old Private JWM. At the Town Hall Court inquest, a fellow soldier said he knew the private and had last seen him at midnight on the 14th September; he had no reason to think he had been drinking but had noticed that he looked unwell and his cap was missing. The witness described the dead man as liking beer, shy but jolly. Private JWM went to his bed in the car park and later witnesses heard a sound, as if some rifles had been knocked over. When another witness went to clean his rifle at about 12.15 pm on the 14th it was missing. He then heard a shot and with other soldiers he ran to the boat house, at the White Rock end of the car park, where he found Private JWM dead, with a gunshot wound to the chest. On a bench there was a rifle, supported by two big tins. This led to the conclusion that the soldier had propped the gun on the tins, leaned over the muzzle of the rifle, reached down to the trigger and shot himself. The Police Pathologist Dr Cordelia Nesbit-Wood, said that the murder victim, an elderly woman in good health, showed signs of having suffered violence, including skull and facial injuries and that she had died from pressure on the neck, about six hours before her body was discovered. The soldier's forage cap was found under the woman's body and a khaki handkerchief and a valise strap, which belonged to him, were nearby. Among Private JWM's possessions were two notes: One said, "Dear Dad, Something came over me this time-there is no other road out-but don't worry, everything is for the best-Bill. The other said: "I am no good to you and never was." Addressing the jury, the Coroner said: "Miss J was found in horrible circumstances which showed a brutal rape had been committed. I cannot help thinking it was the act of a manic." The jury returned a verdict that the soldier had murdered the woman and committed suicide, while of unsound mind. There was not one more word on the tragedy in subsequent editions of the local newspaper- the only murder in WWII Hastings. Even Vigilant remained silent on the matter.

It must have been something of a relief for the court to return to the routine of dealing with the many offenders under wartime regulations. The details of one case, brought to the court in October by the Ministry of Food, may have provided a certain grim delight to the readers of the Hastings and St Leonards Observer. One of the local MOF enforcers seemed over zealous in pursuing his official duties and he was put in his place in a case of a Hastings trader allegedly overcharging. The shop in question was the greengrocer Coopers the Fruiterers, whose speedy and cheerful shop service was their hallmark. The food enforcer visited the shop several times in one afternoon and afterwards claimed that he had been overcharged for potatoes and plums. Under cross examination he began to get a bit above himself and when the defending counsel used the words, I put it to you…The food enforcer replied, "You may put what you like, it does not alter the fact". "How dare you answer counsel like that?" said the defence. "As a retired Metropolitan Police Officer you should know better and if you do it again I shall ask the Bench to reprimand you." To which came the reply, "Do your worst, I shall stick to the truth." The shop owner claimed that if there had been an incident of overcharging it was a mistake and not a calculated ploy. The defending counsel then quoted from a radio broadcast, recently made by the Minister of Food, Lord Woolton: "We do not want to catch people out because they have made a mistake but we do want to catch people who are deliberately overcharging." The defending counsel described the case before the court as "very trumpery" and said that the so-called overcharging was an honest mistake, if a mistake at all and the Ministry of Food's enforcer was out to trap the tradesman in an improper manner. The Bench dismissed the case and declined to make an order for costs.

In November the Coastal Ban was lifted and it came as tonic to the town, as residents anticipated Christmas and family reunions. Other restrictions remained; newcomers could only take up residence for reasons of employment, running a business, to look after a close relative or if they had been certified homeless by another local authority. The sudden lifting of the ban added further to the confusion of regulations. In Hastings Magistrates Court a few weeks later, a man who had just come home from London admitted to being in the curfew area after 10.30pm. He thought that Hastings was now an open town, as he had heard the curfew had been relaxed in some southern coastal towns and thought it applied to Hastings. The man was fined 10/-(50p)

The shortage of petrol or the long-term absence of the only driver, usually male, from the household, resulted in most private vehicles being taken off the road. The government was concerned that in the event of an invasion the enemy would commandeer these vehicles, so everyone owning an unused car or motorcycle was compelled to immobilise it. A road tax rebate could be claimed for the de-licensed vehicle but key parts of it had to be removed, labelled with owner's name and address and deposited at a police station. Drivers who parked their cars for all but the briefest periods were told to remove the rotor arm to disable the vehicle. The man before the court had failed to comply fully with immobilisation regulations; he had removed the battery from the car but the distributor head and leads were still in place. Acting Chief of Police Buddle found this, as almost everything else, "a serious matter", particularly as there had been posters exhibited all over the town, warning motorists of the new regulation. As it was the first of its kind, the bench dismissed the case under the Probation of Offenders Act.

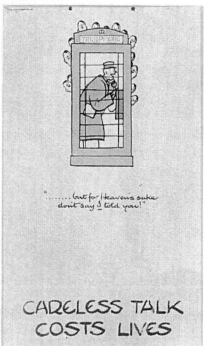

An example of a Fougasse poster

Vigilant seemed to take pleasure in reporting that magistrates in the nearby coastal town of Eastbourne, unlike Hastings, were stiffening their attitude, in sentencing a blackout regulations offender to one month's prison. But his main grouse was under the headline, "Avoidable Waste", with reference to wasting paper. In the autumn of 1941, the government published a fifty-page booklet on the subject of Avoidable Waste, a copy of which was to be delivered free to every household in Great Britain. The book was illustrated by Cyril Kenneth Bird, the Editor of Punch Magazine, who, under the pseudonym Fougasse, created the famous WWII home front propaganda posters. Vigilant said: "I have no quarrel with the subject matter of the book but it is difficult to see how the Ministry of Information is justified in using

paper in this way in order to promote saving it, when appeals to salvage waste paper are also constantly made on the wireless and in the newspapers. The book is in itself a waste of paper and I hope you will waste no time, after reading it, in consigning to the scrap collections." Laudable advice but bearing in mind the shortage of paper of every kind at the time, most copies were probably hung on a string in the lavatory, for more intimate re-cycling!

ACT FOUR 1942

By 1942 the war had torn families apart, the education system had broken down and groups of young friends had been separated by evacuation. In a newspaper article, a Hastings Magistrate, Mr. E T Heron, deplored the inadequate schooling and the level of juvenile delinquency. (The expression "juvenile delinquent' was commonly used in the 1940s and some time after, to describe young offenders). Mr Heron also made strong criticism of the lack of facilities provided by the local education authorities and their failure to keep children out of mischief. Before Hastings Juvenile Court, in early January 1942, was a group of thirteen children, aged 9 to 15 years, charged with shop breaking and larceny. A nine year-old boy was charged with stealing a bottle of proprietary tonic water valued at 4/6d (23p) from a chemist shop and, with the help of others, he had done £10 worth of damage to the chemist's basement storeroom. The probation officer, Miss C. W. Brown, said that the boy had not been to school for 12 months; he was put on probation for a year. A case of breaking and entering was brought against 8 boys and 2 girls, who stole camera cases, film and other property valued at £2 from a High Street shop. The young offenders were given varying periods of probation. Two boys aged 12 and 15 entered a private house in Nelson Road and stole a selection of items; a suitcase, a toy yacht, a satchel and a face mask valued at 10/- (50p). Acting Chief of Police Buddle said it was a sad case: The 15 year old boy was mentally defective and the mother of the 12 year-old had died when he was born and he was now beyond the control of his 72 year old father. An older brother who had looked after the boy very well had been called up. The older offender was remanded for 2 weeks and the younger put on probation for 2 years. Following the comment by Magistrate Heron, an Observer reporter investigated the schooling system and discovered that only 2,700 local children, excluding those at private establishments, were attending school for just three hours daily. The obstacle to re-opening all the schools was the lack of air raid shelters. This problem sprang from the early part of the war: Because Hastings was initially considered a safe reception area for evacuees the government did not allocate large supplies of air raid shelter building materials to the town, as these were regarded as being more urgently needed elsewhere. Therefore, when Hastings became vulnerable after the German invasion of France, there were insufficient shelters throughout the town, including on school premises, so the schools were closed.

Parents of evacuated children were obliged by law to pay towards the upkeep of their absent family; for some the responsibility was too much. Summoned before the court was a father, an Old Town resident, who owed £5.10.6, (£5.55) for the billeting of three of his children. He was earning £3.16.00 (£3.80) per week and in addition he received a disability pension of £ 1.18.00 (£1.90) per week. He had 10 children; six of whom were under ten years old. Prosecutor, Town Clerk Stephen King, said that the majority of parents were making honest endeavours to meet their obligations but a minority was not paying. In fact, the actual amount outstanding in this case was £38; an order for payments of 12/-(60p) a week to clear the debt was made. Even translated into today's values, the family income seems rather inadequate to keep 12 people in rent, food, clothing and other necessities. No wonder the Old Town grocer had rations to spare. It's likely that the defendant's evacuated children were enjoying a higher standard of living elsewhere, with generous hosts supporting them out of their own pockets.

At the end of January there was a further two months extension on the lifting of the ban on persons visiting the coast between Hastings and Littlehampton. Maybe it was this relaxation of regulations that caused an army officer to forget other security measures that were still very much in force. In an unlocked car, he left 7 military maps and he also neglected to remove the rotor arm from the car to immoblise it. Police Constable Cheeseman said he discovered the car at 8.00pm, it was unattended and without a front number plate. The police officer tried to find the owner of the car without success, so he took the rotor arm and maps to the police station. He then kept observation until 10.05pm, when the defendant and another officer came to the car from a nearby cocktail bar. The defendant, who neither appeared in court nor wrote a letter of explanation, was fined £10 for failing to immobilise his vehicle and £2.10.00 (£2.50) for the missing number plate. The reference to a cocktail bar by the police officer hints at the variety of licensed premises in Hastings in WWII: There was a total of 206, which included 19 various kinds of clubs. The licensing of premises for the sale of alcohol and the provision of music and dancing was, and still is, the province of local magistrates. At the February 1942 meeting of the annual Brewster Sessions, the court that oversees licensing matters, the magistrates were pleased to announce a further reduction in the figures for convictions for drunkenness for the year 1941: There were in all 23 cases-17 male and 6 female and only five of these were residents of the town. (If this record of WWII crime seems to give too much importance to drunkenness figures in the forties, it is to contrast the statistics with those of today. In 2003 44% of victims of violence claimed that their attacker was under the influence of alcohol and 70% of night admissions to hospital casualty departments at weekends were linked to drinking). Trade in Hastings wartime licensed premises was no doubt aided by the numbers of British and overseas military personnel billeted in the area. Magistrate Heron had some kind words for these: "Considering the wartime circumstances and the many servicemen here, who are far from family and home comforts, the cases of drunkenness are very few." He complimented the licensees who, in the face of the shortage of supplies, had not been tempted to sell their supplies of drink to privileged customers. It seems that drink had a part to play in a court case involving a young soldier and his civilian friend. The men, both in their early twenties, had been out for a drink and on the walk home decided they would make some extra cash by stealing chickens from Yew Tree Farm, on The Ridge, the property of Mr. Ernest Novis. The civilian offender was engaged on essential work, driving a delivery van and it was in this vehicle that the crateful of 19 chickens, valued at £11.17.6, (£11.78) was transported after the theft. The two men later sold the chickens for £6.10.00 (£6.50) the lot, to witness Alfred Baker and split the proceeds. The unfortunate 18 birds, contained in a crate (one had died in transit) were exhibited in court as evidence in the case and were identified by the farmer. The two defendants came up with conflicting stories as to which of them was to blame for the crime. The magistrates decided that the soldier had led the civilian astray and both were guilty. He made a restitution order for the sum of 12/6d (63p) for the dead chicken and the two men were sentenced to three months hard labour.

There seems to be a fatal connection between chickens and soldiers, demonstrated from a further case in 1942, described in a letter by Victor Bulger, a Canadian soldier stationed in the area. "A farmer near where we were billeted had a few chicken coops and one night my three pals and I went to have a look-see. My pal, MacQueen, put his fingers in the coop, pulled out a squawking chicken, broke its neck and threw it over to me and I stuffed it in a sand bag in short order. He quickly got and killed three more and we took the chickens back to camp, plucked and cleaned them and put them in a pot of boiling water. We had a good feed off them and buried the feathers and bones in a hole in the ground. The army calls this scrounging, not stealing, unless you are caught. We went back to the farm and "scrounged" 21 chickens and hid them in a hedge. The next morning we saw two policemen in the farmer's field and they eventually came to talk to our Troop Commander, Captain Roberts. The police searched our huts, where they found two army tunics, with spots of blood on them; one belonged to MacQueen. While the whole troop was being questioned

Crown Inspection, 1936. The last mounted Constable — P.C. W. T. Paterson on "Kitty".
Left to right :- Mr. J. Bell, Chief Constable; Captain Hyland, Chairman of the Watch Committee, and Superintendent W. J. Buddle.

by the police, MacQueen sneaked back into the hut and scraped the blood off his tunic. He had to appear in court and the camp cook went to give evidence on his behalf, saying that MacQueen had helped him clean some chickens and perhaps that was how the blood got on his clothing. The case was dismissed. A couple of weeks later, MacQueen and me and two other army pals were on town patrol and a fight broke out in a pub, so we went to assist the police, in case any of our regiment was involved. One of the police recognized MacQueen from the stolen chicken court case and jokingly said "Hello Chick!" We all had a good laugh with the police and there were no hard feelings". On

Another great British Salvage campaign

70 MILLION BOOKS COLLECTED

50,000,000 books in 11 months

70,000,000 books in 14 months—up to December 1943

Scrutineers sort the books into three categories...

1 Repulping for munitions

2 Restocking blitzed libraries

3 For Services' reading

the suburban home front many people turned to raising poultry to augment the family food supply. The sound of cockerels crowing was common along residential streets throughout the war and for some years after. Mrs Hammond aged 91, said that during the war she kept chickens for their eggs but even in this backyard farming, regulations came into effect: Householders who kept poultry were only allowed to retain a certain number of eggs for the family's use; the rest had to be surrendered to the authorities. The family also had to forgo its egg ration in exchange for a supply of chicken food, which was also rationed.

As spring approached, Hastings Town Council turned its discussions to the subject of joy-riding and whether the Corporation car should be "labelled", as they termed it. In the forties the expression joy-riding meant pleasure motoring, not the present day crime of the taking away and driving of another's vehicle without their permission. Judging by

"PACKETS?"

"THOSE ARE THE THINGS THAT ARE SHORT"

Many articles can only be sold in containers which are made from waste paper—the paper you may thoughtlessly be burning or throwing away. Please save every scrap of waste paper—it is valuable raw material. For instance, one ton of waste paper makes 15,680 cleansing powder canisters.

★ *Shortage of labour has sometimes made the collection of waste paper difficult, but this problem is now becoming easier —so please save all your waste paper for the collector.*

Issued by the Board of Trade

the amount of weekend visitors to Hastings in local authority cars in the early forties, it was thought by local councillors that other town councils were not particularly scrupulous in the matter of joy-riding. The main vehicle owned by Hastings Corporation was a 1935, 7hp Austin, bought seven years previously, after due consideration of it as an economic proposition. Alderman Tingle thought that to mark the car "Hastings Corporation", with letters of gold leaf would turn the town into a laughing stock. The matter was shelved. The final link with equine police transport was broken in 1942, when the mounted section of the force was disbanded, owing to the wartime shortage of animal feed. The police horse, Kitty, was put out to grass at Pevensey. She enjoyed several years of retirement but unfortunately had to be destroyed, on account of injuries sustained when she fell into a ditch.

The Ministry of Supply Salvage of Waste Order -1942 came into effect on 9th March: Thenceforth it was a punishable offence to burn or destroy waste paper and cardboard, throw it away or dispose of it otherwise than to an authorised collector or buyer. It was also punishable to put waste paper in a refuse bin or mix it with refuse in any way. This order did not encompass confidential or secret documents. These and items like love letters could be sent to an address in Fleet Street, London where, "it will be seen to that they are shredded by a machine and pulped." Government regulations always found the full support of Vigilant, who said that the Salvage of Waste Order was framed with mainly careless housewives in mind but everybody should be careful to salvage their bus tickets and empty cigarette packets. He indulged in some private outrage at a report that the day after the Order came into force, the residents of Clinton Crescent woke up to find, "what was nothing less than a deliberate flouting of the new regulation"; somebody had distributed pieces of paper the entire length of the pavement: "The persons or person, (and I hope there is only one person capable of such a deed), must be either a fool or a traitor. I hope they come before the court and are given a prison sentence." The government reminded shopkeepers that, except in the case of foodstuffs, the wrapping of purchased goods had become illegal and housewives were advised not to go shopping without a basket or a bag and to keep a supply of sturdy brown paper bags to use again and again until they were fit only for salvage.

Even when the shopping was safely home and put away it still was not free from government regulations. The Ministry of Food laid down controls on the amount of food that could be kept in the store cupboard: In a press feature the MOF posed the rhetorical question: "What is hoarding and how much food can you keep in store, without finding yourself on the wrong side of the law? You may keep in stock any amount of rationed food or that which a householder has grown, provided it was obtained legally and is not more than would be needed for four weeks". This law also applied to boarding houses and restaurants.

The Ministry of Food's responsibilities were far-reaching: Its inspectors came to Hastings to oversee a dramatic exercise and test of the effects of poison gas on food. Officials watched a demonstration and training session, during which tear gas and practice mustard gas were poured over condemned fresh meat and tinned food, in an empty shop in the town centre's Robertson Street. The police and a decontamination squad, wearing protective clothing, were on the scene to deal with "casualties" and send them to a cleansing station. Passing bus passengers, who had neglected to carry their gas masks, were seen wiping their eyes, which were streaming from the effect of the tear gas. The food was taken to a football field on the perimeter of the town for cleaning, inspection and testing as part of the exercise.

The present day impression of the WWII home front is of a citizenry that complied with regulations in a spirit of selfless patriotism. Three cases before Hastings Police court proved that even for those involved in emergency, life-saving organisations, personal frustrations could be put before duty. A Civil Defence worker of was stated to have given up his job as a rescue party leader because he was fed up with it and as a skilled worker he felt he was wasting his time. Police Sgt: Kemp said in court that the defendant was the Depot Superintendent of Tower Road Civil Defence Post, a duty from which he was not entitled to be absent without permission. Acting Chief of Police Buddle said that the man was of good character with no previous convictions; as it was the first case of its kind the court imposed a fine of only £1. The second case was heard in the juvenile court, the defendant, a full time messenger with the National Fire Service, was only 16 years old. He failed to turn up for duty because he felt he had lost position in the service by being given a bicycle instead of a motor cycle. (He was described as having a decided bent for mechanics and engineering).The defendant was also unhappy in his job, which involved a lot of waiting about with nothing to do but play snooker. Miss Dorothy Morgan, acting for the boy, admitted the offence. The defendant had joined what was at that time named the Auxiliary Fire Service and was not aware that when the organisation's name was changed to the National Fire Service, in August 1941, messenger boys automatically became firemen and were subject to the laws connected with this role. The Chairman of the Bench warned the boy that if he did not do his duty he would be brought before the court again and be dealt with more severely; the case was dismissed without judgment. The first prosecution for failing to do fire watching took place in Hastings in October 1942. The defendant claimed that he had absented himself from duty to draw attention to the lack of cooperation between the managers of the premises in the sectors under surveillance by his team. He also claimed that there was an inadequate number of fire watchers for the roof area to be watched, which was three times that scheduled for safety. The magistrate said that this was no justification for absenteeism from important duty and if it were, the war effort would stop. The defendant was fined £2.

WASTE THE FOOD
AND
HELP THE HUN

A Hastings girl who represented a very different attitude to duty was Joyce Brewer who started working as a delivery girl for a local milkman in 1940 at the age of 14. She said: "My job wasn't regarded as any kind of National Service as far as I know. Anyhow, at the start of the war I was too young to sign up for anything. I just got on with it, no matter what happened and whatever the weather". By this Joyce means that as well as doing doorsteps deliveries she collected milk from farms, lifting heavy milk churns, often unaided, from the wooden platforms set up at farm gates. She worked alone and later, when she learned to drive, she had to cope with punctures to the van wheels: "It was a chore changing the wheels, which I had to do quite often. New tyres were like gold dust and the retreads soon wore down to the canvas-no rules about minimum treads in those days. There was nobody around to help me jack up the van and manhandle the wheel nuts off and mend punctures. I nearly broke my ankles at times, stamping the tyres back on the rims. We were actually encouraged to do illegal things when driving, like turning off the engine and coasting down hills, to save petrol. Motor vehicles were very basic then, we didn't have steering locks in those days and the windscreen wipers worked off compression from the engine, so when the van was labouring up a steep hill the wipers did not work at all. If the roads were too bad in the snow we often had to resort to sledges or a bike, so off I'd go on an errand boy's old bone shaker, with a crate of milk on the front". Joyce operated her own 'rationing' scheme (perhaps better described as redistribution), with milk supplies, which would have brought down on her the wrath of the Ministry of Food, if they had come to know of it. However, it seems a very intelligent arrangement. Joyce said: "I used to feel sorry for the people who lived alone, because at one time their weekly milk ration went down to 2 pints a week per person, when the cows weren't producing so much milk in the winter. For these people a cup of tea was almost a luxury and milk puddings non existent. So I tried to work something out for them with the large, hard up families, who could not afford their full quota of milk". Joyce also did her bit for the war effort by making sure every milk bottle was returned for re-use.

Others were less public spirited when it came to food supplies, as demonstrated in 1942, when Hastings saw its first prosecution for wasting food. A couple was accused of wasting food over a period of

60 days. The waste, produced in court as evidence, consisted of bread, galantine (meat loaf) fruitcake, scones, muffins and tins of milk, was all discovered in the dustbin of the offenders. In their defence the couple said they were frequently away from home and also ate out a lot and as there was not an efficient system for the collection of waste for pigs, they had put the stale food in the dustbin. The husband was fined two pounds and the wife three pounds.

The theft of pub glasses, increasingly in short supply, was also taken

The wrong and right ways to wait for a bus in wartime

very seriously, as may be gathered from the following examples: "Pub licensees throughout the country are complaining that drinking glasses are disappearing in their thousands and they feel offenders should be fined or sent to prison." said the prosecuting solicitor, Mr. Harold Glenister, at Hastings Police Court, on behalf of the Licensed Victuallers Association. Before the court was a local woman, who had walked out of the King's Head Pub at Ore, taking with her a glass, half-filled with beer, when 'time' was called. The licensee gave chase and apprehended the woman. The said glass, produced in court, was valued at one shilling (5p). The magistrate decided to make an example of her and she was given a fine of two pounds or 14 days in prison.

In April 1942, the Ministry of Transport announced that from the 12th onwards it would be compulsory for bus passengers to: "Form a queue: if six or more people are waiting at a stopping-place." Vigilant, a daily bus traveller, was very keen on the new regulation. "Those who throw cold water on the idea have not had the personal experience of congestion at bus stops that I have endured. In fact, the presence of a police officer, shepherding the crowd, would tend to lessen the chaos and help to see fair play to those who have been waiting longest. Relations between the police and public in Hastings are such that people will happy to cooperate." The Hastings Observer reported: "Though shy at the beginning of the week, when the new regulation on queuing came into force, people soon began to form queues at the main stops round the Memorial." There were, however, many misunderstandings, as travellers jostled for different buses that all pulled in at the same spot but were bound for a variety of destinations. It became clear that a separate stopping place was required for each service. Acting Chief of Police Buddle said the police had been trying to evolve a queuing system since 1926 and the new Order made things no better. Adding to the problem was the fact that a trolley bus cannot draw in ahead of another because of the overhead system. A solution was eventually found; metal railings were erected at various points, at 40 feet intervals, at points round the town centre's Albert Memorial Clock (now demolished) and each bus service was allocated its own stopping place. The method was introduced by Councillor S Riddle, Chairman of the Transport Committee, and he appealed to the public to help make it a success. In May, Hastings had its first prosecution under the new queuing regulations: It was stated in court that: "The defendant took up her position in a queue otherwise than behind the last person forming that queue." After the magistrate pointed out that the maximum sentence for this crime was a fine of £100 or three months in prison, the case was dismissed, with the warning that future offenders would not be treated so lightly.

Acting Chief Buddle, in spite of his important position in the town, was a regular bus user, as can be learned in a story from the widow of bus driver, Cyril Nunn: "One day my husband was driving his bus, full of passengers, down London Road, St Leonards, during an air raid, when the Germans were trying to bomb the railway station. The tall buildings and the narrow street funnelled a huge cloud of debris and dust into London Road, so my husband put his foot down to escape and Mr. Buddle, who was on the bus, was thrown to the floor, along with the other passengers. My husband said to him: "That wasn't very dignified, was it, Sir?" Mr. Buddle obviously bore no ill will because a few months later he saw my husband's bus just clip the new bus queue railings at the town centre and he said: 'I didn't see that Cyril'". Mrs. Nunn continued: "In those days, passengers knew all the bus drivers and conductors personally and appreciated the service they gave. Sometimes, when my husband pulled up at a bus stop next to Whimhurst, the butcher's shop, the boss would run out and give him a pound of sausages. They weren't rationed but were very hard to get if you were not in the shop at the right time".

The appointment of the new Hastings and St Leonards Chief of Police was announced in April as being a Mr. Cargill, aged 35, married with two children. He was formerly of the Liverpool City Police force, where he had rapidly gained promotion. The successful candidate was selected from a final short list of seven that included the Acting Chief, Buddle. Hastings was soon to find that in Cargill, a man of military background and bearing, they had a new style of police chief. The Town Council may have already caught a hint of what was to come, when they debated the appointment; Councillor Rymill found it "amazing" that it was necessary to go outside the town for a new police chief and Councillor Riddle described the appointment as "unfortunate" and wondered, before paying a tribute to Mr Buddle, if it was even the right time to make a change. The salary of the new

Chief was published in the local newspaper; £700 per annum with biennial increments of £50 up to £900. Mr Cargill has been described by his former police colleagues as, "A firebrand with very modern ideas" "One of the finest police chiefs Hastings has ever had". "He was a strict disciplinarian but also very fair". "He might give you a dressing down in private but he always stood up for his men in public". Ex-Police Constable Ken Buddle mentioned a personal detail about Mr Cargill: "He owned a white, Staffordshire bull terrier that he used to take to the police station in his car, when he looked in there at night. On his way home, Mr Cargill would put the dog on the road at the town centre and it had to run after the car for a few hundred yards, along Cambridge Road; that was the dog's exercise. There was not much traffic about at that late hour in those days".

It was evident that the anti-war faction was still at work in Hastings, as can be gathered from a court appearance of a 20 year-old conscientious objector, who had been rejected by the tribunal, and had refused to take

Lewes Prison

a service medical. According to Prosecuting Solicitor Elliott, acting for the Ministry of Labour and National Service, "The defendant has been influenced by older men, who should know better and whose motives, as far as the interest of country are concerned, are not above suspicion." The CO was sentenced to six months in prison, which may have been spent at Lewes Prison, in Sussex. Lewes Prison, as such places go, must have been one of the least welcoming institutions. It was built in 1853 and retained its stark, Victorian atmosphere into the late 1960s, when the conditions there were described as abhorrent. The history of the prison does not appear to be extensively documented but one fact unearthed, which must have brought some satisfaction to its inmates if they heard of it, was that in 1940 the Lewes Prison Governor was arrested and charged with breaking blackout regulations-the case was eventually dropped.

Circumstances relating to the apparent failure of a man to undertake military service were brought to the attention of Vigilant: "I had hoped that we could get through the war without any local examples of incidents that were so common in the early stages of the 1914-1918 War; that of presenting white feathers to men not wearing service uniform. A RAF man, on leave and wearing civilian clothing, was given an envelope containing four white feathers- he treated the act with amused contempt. I hope we will have no more of this detestable nonsense in Hastings. White feather distributing is usually carried out by hysterical and possibly deranged females. I suggest they volunteer for the women's services, whose members would not indulge in such cheap behaviour". He also deplored the towns' rumour mongers, who had been circulating false stories that because of military, Home Guard and Civil Defence training exercises to be held in town on Saturday, 13th June 1942, all normal life would be suspended and nobody could shop, go to the cinema, or pursue any outdoor activity. In the following week, the new Chief Constable Cargill, interviewed two people who had publicly made statements of an alarmist nature that were totally unfounded. Mr. Cargill gave the persons interviewed some sound advice on the matter of spreading rumours and warned that future cases of the kind would face prosecution.

Vigilant was jubilant: "I propose a vote of thanks to Chief Constable Cargill; we have been plagued in this town by half-truths, sometimes

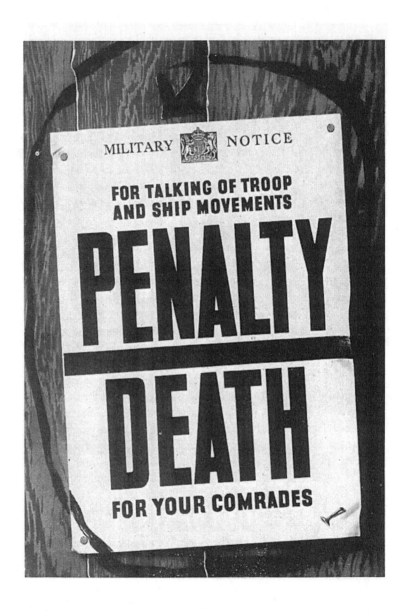

circulated by people of standing, who should know better. Mr. Cargill has put the wicked trade in rumour in its right place-as a punishable offence." It may have been one of these half-truths from Hastings' war years that re-surfaced in 2003, in a letter published in the Daily Mail, on the subject of an attempted invasion of England. The letter, from a man who had visited relatives in Hastings as a child in 1940, recounted that it was local talk at the time that a small task force of German soldiers had been repelled and burned alive by the process of igniting oil that was poured on the sea. The charred remains of some of the dead were said to have been washed up on Hastings beach. Research indicates that no such incident occurred and it is more probable that the charred bodies were from burning ships that were sunk in the channel. There was certainly oil, stored in huge tanks near the seafront, to be used to repel an invasion but it was never used. But of such stuff are rumours made!

Cases of looting increased: Two men, posing as being in need of a flat to rent in Hastings obtained keys of unoccupied properties from estate agents and then proceeded to remove the flats' contents and sell them to local second-hand dealers, which proved to be the looters' undoing. Several dealers notified the police and the shop owners were later able to identify the thieves, one of whom, when trying to sell a fishing rod to the angler's shop, Redfearns, falsely claimed to have been invalided out of the army, after Dunkirk. His accomplice was described by prosecuting counsel as a plausible and cunning thief, both had previous convictions. One was given six months hard labour the other three months in prison, with as much hard labour as his physical condition would allow. In another case, a mother and her underage daughter, over a period of time, removed and sold the contents of an absent neighbour's house. The mother was given six months hard labour and the daughter was sent to an approved school.

A new regulation from the Ministry of Supply was announced in July: Henceforth it would be the responsibility of cobblers to decide to what extent a pair of shoes needed to be repaired. The leather and rubber used by cobblers was imported and these materials were more urgently needed for military footwear. Supplies for mending civilian shoes were to be restricted and full sole repairs were no longer permitted, just the patching of worn areas, with a small piece of leather. Many people resorted to mending their own shoes. Scrap textiles had also become precious, so when a Hastings Corporation worker was found in possession of a sack of waste fabric, valued at one shilling, (5p) he was taken to the police station and later to court. Further investigation revealed he owned a garage that contained three tons of waste textiles, which the defendant said he had bought as off-cuts from clothing manufacturers, tailors and, "a one-armed man at South Terrace." As the defendant was neither a registered scrap dealer nor an authorised salvage collector he was fined £15 for stealing salvage and only escaped prison because of his previous good character.

A new offence was added to the Lighting Act with the introduction of the Waste of Fuel Order: A woman was summoned for displaying a light and wasting electricity. Police Constable Cheeseman said that at 10.20pm he saw a light coming from a house in Priory Street and,

On Active Service

Electricity delivers the goods

Tanks to be shipped to the battlefronts . . . guns to be moved . . . supplies to be sent forward . . . Electricity is on the job — lifting, carrying, maintaining communications. That is why WE MUST SAVE FUEL TODAY.

unable to get a reply, he broke in and found and extinguished a 60watt bulb in the unoccupied house. The woman, who claimed that the light had not been on for more than five hours, was fined 10/- (50p). The same fine was handed down to a woman who left a light on in a public convenience at the Fishmarket. Another, who was summoned for wasting electricity, told the magistrate that she had gone to bed early for a fortnight to make up for what she had wasted.

The first prosecution under the Misuse of Petrol, Motor Fuel Rationing (3) Order, occurred at the end of August. People who received special allowances for essential purposes were obliged to use that petrol only for the purpose for which it was granted. This scheme was brought to an end on 30th June 1942 and any remaining supplies of basic petrol allowance were to be used up by 31st July. In court, Chief of Police Cargill accepted the defendant's explanation that the petrol that he used to go to church on 2nd August was some that he had in hand. However, under the new regulation he should have applied for a special license to use it. A nominal fine of ten shillings (50p) was imposed. The confused churchgoer was not the only one to fall foul of the complexities of the plethora of wartime regulations on the use and supplying of petrol: A kindly deed brought two traders to court, on the mutual offence of supplying and using petrol, other than that obtained from an authorised dealer in motor fuel. One man had applied to the authorities for extra petrol for a journey to be made on a special day. Verbal permission for the supply had been granted to him but the written confirmation had not arrived by the appointed day, so he borrowed a gallon from another trader, undertaking to return it. Mr. Cargill said that he viewed the case very seriously: "Motorists must realize that the regulations must be strictly complied with and trafficking in petrol is not allowed". Both men said that they had no intention of breaking the law; it was just a case of doing a fellow trader a good turn. The Chairman of the Bench, Mayor, Doctor W E Jameson, said that the case had been very properly brought and fined the defendants one pound each.

Earlier in the year, Magistrate Mr. E T Heron had complimented the soldiers billeted in the town for their lack of drunkenness in spite of being far from family and home comforts. But there was one "home comfort" that some serving men were not willing to forgo. At Hastings Police Court a married woman appeared for keeping a disorderly house and allowing a person under 16 (in this case a fourteen and a half year-old girl) to frequent the same. In law, this quaint expression, 'disorderly house' indicates a dwelling in which: "The conduct of its inmates is such as to become a public nuisance or a house where persons congregate to the probable disturbance of the public peace or other commission of crime". In England, under the Disorderly Houses Act 1751, the term included common bawdy houses or brothels and "the keeping of such a house is a misdemeanour, punishable by fine or imprisonment".

Hastings Police had been keeping watch on the house in question for nearly a week. One of the officers was Policewoman Sergeant Doris Sterry, who stated that during her observation she was: "Approached by about half a dozen fellows who were looking for the house". The police eventually entered the property and found an 18 year old girl in a bed and two soldiers, sitting on chairs in the same room; the girl

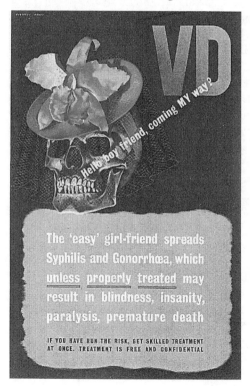

The 'easy' girl-friend spreads Syphilis and Gonorrhœa, which unless properly treated may result in blindness, insanity, paralysis, premature death

IF YOU HAVE RUN THE RISK, GET SKILLED TREATMENT AT ONCE. TREATMENT IS FREE AND CONFIDENTIAL

admitted to sleeping with soldiers but claimed she never received any money. A witness, the girl's younger brother, said in court that he had peeped through a gap in the blackout and seen his sister in bed with a soldier. The married woman said that because she was alone in the house with her baby, the fourteen and a half year-old girl was there to keep her company but she did not know what the girl did in the house during her visits. When charged with keeping a disorderly house the woman said: "Never, these men are my friends, who came to play cards". The defendant pleaded for leniency because of her 9 month-old baby; she was sentenced to one month's hard labour. The public was made sharply aware of the health risks in using such premises or indulging in promiscuity by a number of hard-hitting, Ministry of Information posters. By 1943 the total incidence of venereal disease was 139% higher than in 1939, a situation which posed a threat to the war effort.

Ex-Inspector Banks recounted his memories of Woman Police Officer Sterry mentioned in the disorderly house case: "Sergeant Doris Sterry was nicknamed The Beauty of Bath, like the apple, as that was her hometown. After retiring from the force she went to New Zealand and was joined there by Chief Inspector Attwood of the Hastings force, whom she married. Whilst in the Hastings Force, Doris Sterry had the support of Woman Police Sergeant Ethel Tucknott, a very efficient and active officer, who lived at Silverhill. One of Ethel's many successful arrests was that of a flasher in Alexandra Park. She was walking in the park on a rest day, dressed in civilian clothes, when the offender exposed himself to her and fled. Ethel, a very strong and powerful woman, caught him after a long chase; she was trained in Judo and quickly subdued the offender. On another occasion she arrested two men who were drunk and disorderly in the town centre and she took them into Hastings Central Police Station single-handedly, with their heads clamped under her arms, as they struggled and shouted! Ethel Tucknott later served as British Police Officer in the Cyprus insurrections and came under fire several times. She was awarded a decoration for meritorious service by the Governor of Cyprus. She ended her career with the Birmingham City Police and later married a widower, Police Sergeant Bob Tester of the Hastings Force.

A search through any British local paper shows that during wartime the most frequent cause of Magistrate's Court appearances was the breaking of blackout regulations; it was also the cause of a wide variety of explanations and excuses: A man, who was to be married the next day, had overnight guests, who were not familiar with the household's blackouts and they had allowed light to escape. The magistrate, Mr. Heron, said: "This is rather a sorry start for your marriage; instead of giving you a wedding present the court will give you a fine of ten shillings" (50p). At another court hearing, which concerned the validity of an accusation of allowing light to escape, the defendant claimed that the supposed breach of regulations was in fact caused by the moon being reflected in a pane of glass, which had brown paper glued to the inside. Another defendant insisted that the light showing from his house had turned itself on, as a result of a loose wire that had made a connection when the fragile walls of his room vibrated, as people walked up the stairs. His explanation was dismissed as nonsense by the magistrate.

Readers of the book, Letters from Lavender Cottage, will be surprised that even the sedate occupants of this now famous house fell foul of wartime regulations, as shown by this recently discovered letter:

Lavender Cottage,   19th December 1942
The Ridge,
Hastings.

Dear Marion,

We have been having rather an upsetting time of late, all thanks to James, our cat. One night last month something must have attracted him to the window and he got behind the blackout arrangements to investigate and in so doing, he disturbed the curtains. We were totally unaware that there was a light showing until there was a loud banging on the door and there stood a neighbour, Mr Bailey, who is the Air Raid Warden.   He came into the cottage and quoted us an alarming rigmarole of regulations and told us we would probably have to appear in court. He tends to be somewhat officious and he appeared to be rather enjoying his situation.

We were terribly shocked; as you know, we three lead such a quiet life together. Our house companion, poor little Edith Lake, who is the registered householder under war regulations, was quite incapable of going to the court; she was in tears at the mere mention of it. So my friend, Clare, said she would represent us. She dismissed my offer to stand up in court, saying that I might be tempted to make one of my supposedly witty remarks and so alienate the magistrates.

Clare and I went into town by bus on the appointed day and I sat in the court's public gallery, to give moral support. It seems that Mr Bailey had been very busy that night, as he had caught several people, including the owner of the Netherwood Guest House, which is across the road from our cottage. The owner claimed he had not broken the law because the light showing was in truth moonlight, reflected in a window pane. The magistrate would have none of it and the man was fined two pounds!

Clare did not look in the least nervous when she stood before the magistrate. I thought she looked very dignified. She explained about James and the curtain but the magistrate said: "Madam, if I were to accept every story of the antics of cats when it comes to blackout regulations I would come to believe that half the felines in Hastings are in the pay of the enemy!" Some people in the court tittered; it was rather shaming for Clare. We were fined one pound. We did not stay long down the town after that. Everywhere there looks so drab; it's not at all like the place we used to know.

My dear, I am sorry to send you such dramatic news. We are almost recovered from it all now but we will be keeping a very close eye on James in future.

Very much love to you,

Emilie.

Vigilant put a challenging question in his comment column: "Is it an honour to be a Justice of the Peace?" His own view was that having JP after one's name was not in any way to be compared with such letters as GM, DSO or OBE or any similar decoration. He continued: "The modest will not regard the title as an honour but see it as a symbol of an honourable opportunity to serve their fellow men. May I hope that they will also acknowledge when the time has come for them to lay down that service, so that the magisterial benches may be free of the reproach of senility?" He did not, of course, add, "If the cap fits wear it!" It's likely that the shortage of younger candidates, due to wartime conditions, kept many magistrates in the post long after their faculties had started to let them down. It has been documented in Letters from

Lavender Cottage that the magistrate, Countess Brassey, had such a weak voice that it was almost impossible to hear her when she spoke in public and Ex-Police Constable Manklow recalled that another of the magistrates was so severely deaf that he had to: "Use an ear trumpet as big as one of the old gramophone horns. It was the job of one of the officers on duty in the court to shout into the trumpet, when the magistrate misheard a point of law or a piece of evidence". Some doubt has been thrown on the veracity of this anecdote but it is certainly true that one of the wartime magistrates had a serious hearing problem.

The offending trolley bus driver from the 1940 fraud case seemed to have a considerably younger counterpart, when the local paper reported, almost as light relief from the war, "An Amazing Story". Before the juvenile court, "in need of care and protection" was a fourteen and a half year old boy, who was discovered to be living an opulent life at the expense of a lady he had duped. "The boy had been making trips to London three times a week, regularly used taxis, bought the best seats in the cinema, ate six or seven tubs of ice cream during the performance and was smoking big fat cigars and generally spending money like water", said Detective Sergeant Pike, who had apprehended the boy in the cinema. The boy's guardian, when told it was thought that the boy had stolen the money, refused to give the police her assistance. When he was questioned by the police, the boy said he had borrowed the money on behalf of his "uncle", from a lady in St Leonards, which she confirmed. He had told this lady that his "uncle", a titled man, had been robbed and needed money. Over a period of three weeks she gave him a total of £75 for his "uncle". Sergeant Pike said in court: "He is not a bad boy but he does not appreciate what he has done". The young defendant was described as backward and as having done no work since he left school (normally at age 14 in 1942). He was remanded for a medical report.

Nothing further was reported on this extraordinary case, it seems to have been forgotten, as Hastings was gripped by the story of a local baby being stolen from his pram. On the 9th October 1942, the baby's mother, Mrs. S, called in at the Wellington Square Infant Welfare Centre, to collect a supply of tinned milk. Leaving her baby, Robert, in his pram, in the centre's entrance hall, she remained inside for a few minutes to have a cup of tea. When she emerged the pram was empty. The police immediately instituted enquiries; the Welfare Centre Superintendent said that in the 25 year history of the centre nothing of this nature had ever happened. On the following Saturday, the 17th October, the local paper announced the baby had been returned after a 24 hour absence, well fed and cared for. The background to the child stealing offence was both bizarre and tragic. The woman charged with

Happy Reunion

MOTHER AND BABY TOGETHER AGAIN

the offence at Hastings Police Station was Mrs. L, aged 39, who lived in a basement flat in Wellington Square. On Friday 9th October, the woman had instructed an 11 year-old girl, Nellie, known as her step-daughter, to go to the welfare centre and find a baby, a boy if possible, and bring it home. Nellie said that the accused had told her to take along an old pram, used for carrying coal and to put a piece of cloth, a pillow and a shawl inside it. Nellie said," I was frightened and knew it was wrong and I should not do it but I did, or Mother would grumble. Mother was glad to have the baby. She put it in a cradle and when it cried she put it in her bed. The next day, when the story of the stolen baby was in the paper, Daddy told Mother to take the baby to the police station and I went too". On searching the flat, the police found small, wet patches on the woman's bed and damp, stained baby garments, in a bath under the sink. During her first interview at the police station the accused said she was expecting a baby in two weeks time but she was diagnosed as not pregnant by the police doctor. The accused spoke of her passionate fondness for children and said that she thought she should adopt one. Mrs. L was committed for trial at Sussex Assizes, at Lewes. The case came to court in early December. In summing up, Mr. Justice Croom-Johnson said that it was a sad case of a woman who craved a child of her own, "Which is all very well but thought must be given to the anguish of the real mother". The defendant, described as being of good character but of a weak mentality, married in 1932 but separated from her husband. She had worked as a railway carriage cleaner and a street newspaper seller. In the past five years she had lived with three men, including the present one, who was already married. On four different occasions she had claimed to be pregnant. His Lordship said that the proper punishment for the crime was six to twelve months in prison but bearing in mind the defendant's written statement, this sentence would be reduced to three months, of which she had already served six weeks on remand.

On a September Sunday in 1942 an opportunity was given to the members of the Hastings Special Constabulary Reserve to take control of Hastings and St Leonards for 8 hours, without the aid of regular police personnel. Chief of Police Cargill said that he was satisfied that in the event of an emergency the Reserve was completely capable of policing the borough; before the war, the specials had already undergone training and worked ordinary police beats. Cargill described them as efficiently trained and ready to turn out day or night. It was the daily custom, before going on duty for police officers to parade in the Constable's Day Room with their baton, handcuffs and report book in hand. Ex-Inspector Banks explained the normal beat routine: "The police officer on the beat carried out community policing in the old-fashioned way. There were 18 night beats and 17 day beats in the borough and they were walked in alternate reverse order, on odd and even dates. The entrance to every business was inspected twice during a night beat and householders could inform the police of their intended absence, secure in the knowledge that their home was under police supervision while it was empty. With the evacuation of so many families in wartime it became impossible to continue this practice. Punctuality on the beat at all times was obligatory, almost regardless of the circumstances". The Ridge, some six miles from Hastings town centre, although part of the borough, was wild and remote and the police nicknamed it The Klondike. The beat for The Ridge began at St Helen's Police Station (now demolished) on the corner of The Ridge and Winchelsea Road; the first report point was the police box, which was situated opposite to the cemetery gates, at the top of Elphinstone Road. This beat, exposed and 500 feet above sea level, was testing in snowy or wet weather. It included muddy and potholed roads, farms and isolated properties. Some of these, for example, Sandrock Hall, (now demolished) Ore Place and Hurst Court were requisitioned for military purposes in WWII. Police officers had to be fit to cope with the gruelling beats routine and they were expected to attended weekly PT and drill sessions, as a part of their duties. The police force also had a number of other sports activities and Ex-Inspector Banks was the captain of the rifle club.

Ex-Police Constable Manklow recounted a night duty on the Ridge during the war. His ability to drive gave him the advantage of not always having to do the beat on foot. Patrolling constables had been instructed to keep a special eye on a large, empty house in Grange Road, an unmade, residential road just off The Ridge, as looting of slates, wood and other building materials from the property had been going on. As Ex-Police Constable Manklow drove past the house, he saw a flash of light, reflected on metal. He searched the area on foot for some time but could not find anybody, so he decided to conceal himself in the police box and wait. After some time, he heard footsteps approaching so he jumped out and grabbed the passer by. It proved to be a young Coldstream Guard, who confessed that it was him hanging around the house in Grange Road. He was in a distressed state and said he had had enough of the war and he couldn't go on anymore. Ex-Police Constable Manklow took pity on him and instead of charging him with loitering with intent or viewing him as a potential deserter he took him into the police station on a charge of being absent without leave.

On the 24th September 1942, the Gayton Hotel, a private establishment in Hastings, was damaged in an air raid and 4 people were killed. One fortunate woman was not at home when the raid occurred but on her return she found that a gold bracelet, a ring and chain, valued at £20, were missing from a locked cupboard in her bed-sitting room and a police investigation was instigated. It was discovered three weeks later that a Canadian soldier had sold a gold bangle for 2/6d (25p) that matched the description of the one stolen, to a woman in a pie shop; she was later able to identify the soldier. At Hastings Police Court the soldier said that he had found the bracelet in a pile of burned mattresses and brick rubble, on the pavement in front of the Gayton Hotel; he also admitted to having the ring and chain in his possession. It emerged in evidence that the soldier had been part of an army unit, which carried out rescue work at the Gayton hotel. The magistrate told him: "You are a disgrace to your regiment", and gave him a sentence of three months hard labour. There were two Canadian Regiments billeted in Hastings in WWII. One was the Princess Louise Dragoon Guards; it is believed that some soldiers in this regiment had been released from prison to serve in the army and they may have had a less than noble attitude to military service. Ex-Inspector Banks recalls they certainly kept the police busy with their brawls and general disorder. The other regiment in Hastings was the 17th Hussars, 7th Reconnaissance Regiment, who were stationed on the Hastings seafront, mainly in requisitioned hotels. During a daylight raid, on 23rd May 1943 at 1.00pm, a bomb demolished the Albany Hotel and of its Canadian military occupants, 11 were killed and 34 were injured. It must be emphasized that generally the Canadians were very well liked in Hastings and that they are still remembered with affection.

ACT FIVE 1943

The impression of life on the home front in 1943 was one of bleakness. The propaganda that conveyed the message that every individual could have some effect on the war effort was seen everywhere. Advertising hoardings were taken over to promote government drives on saving money, public transport and food. Vigilant wrote a stern message to Hastings on the subject of wasting bread: "Don't help the German U-

Grim messages on the home front

boats! Merchant seamen are the bravest men in the world, who bring us wheat for bread, while under the constant risk of attack from the German U-boats, hunting in packs. What does this mean to you? Do you think of this when you take a slice of bread when you are not really hungry? Do you throw away bread when it is not quite as fresh as it was, eat bread instead of potatoes and waste the crusts from toast? Saving bread helps fight the Battle of the Atlantic". Another commodity was also showing signs of drying up; 50 of Hastings and St Leonards' licensed premises had closed down for the duration of the war and a further three had been damaged by enemy action. The figures on drunkenness in the town fell further, with the previous year's statistics showing that only 8 people had been arrested for being drunk and disorderly, seven male, one female; five of these were non-residents. Alcohol was, of course, still available: It was a case of making the punishment fit the crime, when a woman with two previous convictions appeared before the Hastings Police Court, charged with being drunk and incapable in Robertson Street, at 8.55pm on a Saturday. Police Constable Finch said that the woman, who could hardly stand without assistance, was in possession of a half bottle of gin when arrested. She was fined ten shillings (50p) and the Clerk of the Court, Colonel F G Lanham said that the bottle would be kept as part of the fine.

The heaviest air raid attacks on Hastings occurred during 1943; the civilian population struggled with hazardous war duties that they never thought would fall upon them as private citizens, firewatching being one of these. Ex-Police Constable Manklow was sent out to a Fairlight community, where a group of firewatchers was attempting to deal with a big blaze. The firewatchers were sheltering behind gorse bushes with buckets of water and stirrup pumps, ineffectually spraying the flames, as their leader shouted commands. All were totally unaware that near the cliff edge, some feet behind them, lay a live German sea mine. Police Constable Manklow was unable to give this incident a date but it seems to tally with details of the crash of a German aircraft that occurred on the evening of 4th January 1943. A Dornier 217 flew in from the sea at low level under bad visibility and crashed into the rising ground at Furze Hill, Fairlight. The bomber smashed through an empty bungalow and broke up and burst into flames. Wreckage was strewn over 50 yards, along with the bodies of the German crew of four, leaving only the rear fuselage, tail and engines relatively intact. The fire party's attempts to douse the petrol flames, amid exploding cannon shells, were unsuccessful and it was left to the National Fire Service to bring the blaze under control. Later, local residents sat to be photographed on what they believed to be the planc's fuel tank, unaware that it was the unexploded sea mine!

In the book, Bombers Over Sussex-1943-1945, the writers remark that contrary to normal practice, the four dead airmen from this crash were taken to Folkestone for burial, instead of being interred locally. The explanation for this change of practice may be that in early January 1943, the local press was covering a story about the people of Northiam, a village some miles outside Hastings, who were protesting

YOUR COURAGE
YOUR CHEERFULNESS
YOUR RESOLUTION

WILL BRING

US VICTORY

at the prospect of having dead Nazis buried in their churchyard.

Major changes in the police force took place on 1st April 1943. The scheme was a Home Office wartime measure, under Defence Regulations, to amalgamate all the police forces of Sussex, encompassing the counties of East and West Sussex and the boroughs of Eastbourne, Brighton and Hastings. The reason for the amalgamation was to improve military-police coordination, in connection with the planned invasion of Europe. Hastings was to become the headquarters of Number 2 District of the new police force, with Mr. Cargill as its Assistant Chief Constable. The measure would only be continued after the war by further legislation; it was brought to an end in 1947.

An estate agent's accommodation racket was uncovered by an outraged local serviceman, who found that bombed-out residents, desperately seeking a replacement home, were becoming victims of what today would be called gazumping. The informant wrote to the local paper: "I needed a new home for my family, after ours was bombed and we agreed with the estate agent to pay a rent of 25 shillings (£1.25) per week for a house. The agent then said he had another client for the property but if I agreed to a rent of thirty shillings (£1.50) I could still have the house. I refused to participate in such a swindle. I was then offered a smaller place for 23/- (£1.22) but then I overheard the agent saying on the telephone that he would not let the property for that price and it must be increased to thirty shillings, because there is such a demand for houses after a raid. It seems to me this is a racket that should be exposed. I have been in the army for three and a half years and I did not know such ghouls existed among civilians". If the outraged soldier had had the time to sit in the Hastings Police Court he would have seen that swindles connected with wartime conditions existed in other Hastings businesses. A Ministry of Food Inspector sat at a window above a garage and kept a fourteen and a half hour watch on a café across the road. The proprietor had previously been summoned for not keeping a record of the rationed foodstuffs he had obtained. He said he had surrendered his books to the Food Office, where, he claimed, he was told the government order to keep such records was no longer in force and the books were sent for salvage. He was directed by the court at his first appearance to keep records in future. When the café proprietor came to court again it was stated that during the MOF Inspector's long watch he counted the customers who entered the café (217) and these numbers were matched against the meals, snacks and beverages listed as served during that period; these far exceeded the customers observed entering the premises, the meals alone totaling 436! The café proprietor was fined £7 under the Food Rationing Order. This example of the responsibility of business owners to keep detailed records of their wartime customers applied to many trades. Guests arriving at hotels and boarding houses were obliged, under a war emergency law, to complete forms with their correct name, address and other details. This law often exposed couples who were masquerading as married and could lead to an appearance in court. A lance corporal came to Hastings with a married woman, who posed as his wife and they stayed in a double bedroom in a hotel in Pevensey Road. The woman claimed to be ignorant of the fact that her companion had signed her name as his, although she was standing beside him at the time. The soldier admitted signing the form and making a false statement and said the woman had nothing to do with the filling in of the forms. It came out in evidence that the woman had previously been bound over for housebreaking and larceny and neglecting her children. Mr. Cargill said that the soldier, who had been awarded the BEM for gallantry, had been a victim of circumstances in this case; he was fined £2. The woman was sentenced to three months hard labour for aiding and abetting the man and one month for using a false name, the sentences to run concurrently.

The magnitude of military deserter and failure-to-register statistics were for the most part concealed during the war but at times they reached epidemic proportions. But deserting was not an easy option; unless the offender could find someone willing to collude in his law-breaking he was forced to live on his wits, either doing work of a lowly nature or turning to a life of crime, in order to survive. He became an outlaw, as his lack of identity card or the correct papers could betray him. A case of concealing a deserter came before Hastings Magistrates' Court in May 1943. The offence was discovered when Police Sergeant Cheal visited a house in Parker Road, where he found a soldier living with a married woman, whose husband was serving with the forces. In court the woman said that she believed the soldier was on leave, although he had been in her house for several weeks.

She was sentenced to three months hard labour. At one period in the war there were over 24,500 men wanted for desertion and at the end of 1941 the government ordered a campaign to flush them out. The problem of desertion continued after the war, when there were still over 19, 000 absentees.

Vigilant, who rarely commented on sartorial matters, wrote: "The war is delivering men from the tyranny of clothes: A speaker at one of the Hastings Religion and Life meetings had appeared on the platform wearing a brown suit! The speaker felt it was not necessary to apologise for his attire; if the audience had seen his black suit they would know it was fit for wear only as old clothing. He added that there is no reason why clerics should always be sombre in funereal black". Shabby and inappropriate dress had become respectable. The clothes rationing scheme saved shipping space and left more capacity for the importation of essential materials. The 45,000 men and women released from manufacturing civilian clothing were re-deployed in making uniforms for the armed forces.

Wartime conditions and the new regulations gave many opportunities to those with criminal inclinations. Before Hastings Magistrates' Court was a 21 year old RAF man, married and the father of two children, who was accused of making a statement contrary to the War Damage Act, by attempting to obtain £600 by false pretences. The claim was for his furniture and chattels, which had supposedly been damaged by enemy action while they were in a repository. The defendant had joined the RAF in the early part of the war and, as his family had been evacuated, he had put his furniture and effects in store in a warehouse in St Leonards, which was damaged by enemy action on October 17th 1942. The warehouse owner wrote to the defendant to inform him that the building had been bombed and that he should consider his belongings destroyed and file an insurance claim. A large amount of the stored contents and the documents relating to them were certainly destroyed, but the area containing the defendant's furniture was not badly affected and his goods were salvaged in varying conditions. The defendant made a detailed claim against the government's free insurance scheme but when the warehouse was cleared, doubt was thrown on whether the value of some of the items for which he had claimed were correct, or if they even existed at all. A set of Dickens' works proved to be one copy of a book by Charles Dickens, which was obtained by sending off coupons, cut from a daily newspaper. A claim was made for a dress suit, valued at 8 guineas, (£8. 40p), which the defendant had never owned. He admitted later that some of the prices of his goods were from his own imagination, as certain of the lost items had been gifts; the damaged furniture was being bought on hire purchase. The defendant said he had suffered a run of bad luck for the past five years and admitted to living beyond his means. He had borrowed £50 for a deposit on his house. In his defence he said "I have lost my home but I never intended to make a false claim. Perhaps I filled in the form carelessly but I expected to be able to discuss it with the government assessor, to arrive at a fair value". Pleading leniency, his solicitor, Mr Percy Idle, said: "The absolute stupidity of the whole thing is that the defendant could never have claimed £600, as the government insurance scheme is limited to settlements of no more than £350". The Bench decided that it was a most serious and flagrant case and must be penalized because of its magnitude. A sentence of six weeks in prison was passed and Chairman of the Bench, Mr. Heron said: "We have treated you leniently; you could have received a fine of £100 with three months in prison. I hope this case will be a lesson to others, who may attempt to make claims of this character, that they cannot do so without penalty".

During WWII, an aggressive tax, called the War Damage Contribution, was operated. This tax, introduced by the Inland Revenue, was mainly collected by means of deduction from employment pay. The Collector of Taxes for the Hastings district was Mr Elliot Oscar Eplett. He obtained hundreds of summonses against War Damage Contribution defaulters. The summonses were served by the police and required the defaulter to: "Show cause why the tax had not been paid". Often proceedings terminated in a Distress Warrant being issued by the court, authorizing the seizure of the defaulter's possessions, such as furniture, to be sold for the payment of the tax. The revenue from the War Damage Contributions Tax provided a strictly limited compensation for bomb-damaged property. During the war, insurance companies did not issue policies that covered war risks.

A young couple, who adamantly refused to separate their rubbish and threw away paper and rags mixed in with general waste, came before the court in August 1943, under the Salvage of Waste Order, 1942. They had been repeatedly warned about ignoring the order by the salvage collectors, who eventually reported them to the authorities. Both offenders said it was against the dictates of their conscience to comply, as the salvaged materials were to be used for making weapons of war. The husband followed the Quaker religion and his wife shared his beliefs and views. The man's solicitor, Mr. Morgan said: "He does all he can to save life; he is a member of the hospital first aid party, a fire watcher and the secretary of the Famine Relief Committee but it is against his principles to save materials that can be used for taking life. The couple was bound over for twelve months, after being told that should they repeat the offence, they would be brought before the court again for judgment.

A dispute about ownership of a quantity of waste food destined for pig swill brought two men to the Police Court in a case of assault. In Barley Lane, one Hastings man

TO ALL CAREFUL HOUSEWIVES

THANK YOU

"PAPER!
It means more Ammunition to me."

"METAL!
It means more Guns to me."

"BONES!
They mean more Planes to me."

Put out bones, metal and paper. Put them out separately by your dustbin.

It's not always easy to remember that every scrap counts—but it's true. Every scrap *does* count.

We've started well, so keep it going—keep your friends interested—send suggestions to your local council. You are working for victory.

UP HOUSEWIVES AND AT 'EM!"

ISSUED BY THE MINISTRY OF SUPPLY

encountered the other, who was driving a pony and cart, which was full of waste food. An altercation arose, because one man accused the other of stealing waste that was rightfully his, as he had the contract to collect it from Barley Lane. During the heated exchange that followed, the assailant pulled the driver of the cart by his collar, out of his seat and onto the load of foul-smelling waste. The aggrieved party decided to take the matter to court but in the ensuing days he had received a written apology, which arrived on the morning of the court appearance, so the case still had to be heard. The plaintiff was obliged to pay 14/- (70p) costs.

A 17 year-old boy, who posed as a naval rating, was subsequently charged with unlawfully taking upon himself the designation of leading seaman in the Royal Navy. He had knocked on a woman's front door in Castledown Avenue, dressed in what looked like naval uniform. He told the woman that he was a leading seaman, aged 22 and that he had slept all night on the West Hill cliffs, after having quarrelled with his father, to whom he had given all his leave money. Out of sympathy the woman gave him five shillings. Detective Sergeant Pike said that he saw the accused at his home later that day; he was still wearing the fake naval uniform. When charged with the offence at the police station the 17 year-old said he had done it to try to get back in the services. He explained that when he was 15 he had joined the army but his father got him out of it 18 months later. He had slept out on the cliffs on the occasion in question because his father had threatened him with his Home Guard rifle. The prisoner was remanded in custody.

Chief of Police Mr. Cargill found himself caught up in a drama when he was able to give "prompt and valuable assistance" in the rescue of the crew of two Flying Fortresses that had downed in the sea off Pevensey, close by Hastings. Mr. Cargill was driving past the location when he saw a boat about to go to the rescue of the American airmen. He helped get the flyers aboard the rescue boat and aided one who was lying injured in a dinghy. It was reported that the airmen were in high spirits when they learned that they had been brought ashore at the spot where William the Conqueror had landed in 1066.

Five Hastings fishermen, one of them almost 80 years old, appeared in court; they had been spotted by a War Reserve Police officer, as they went beyond the permitted area of the beach. Their purpose in going onto the beach was to dig for lug worms as bait but the 80 year old said that he had been tempted to do some beach combing to augment his meagre pension. He promised not to offend again. Another fisherman said he was searching the beach to reclaim any valuable fishing equipment that might have been washed ashore. The magistrates decided not to record a conviction and gave no penalty, telling the defendants that there were reasons for the restrictions and they must be respected.

Courtesy of the Editor of the Hastings and St Leonards Observer, the Chief Constable of Sussex, Mr. J. F. Ferguson issued a front page warning on the subject of bicycle theft: "Every year thousands of pedal cycles are reported stolen; in 1936 the picture for England and Wales was 25,000 but in 1941 it was 55,000. During that year, in Sussex alone, 1,700 thefts of bicycles were reported. Due to the war, there are now not enough cycles to go round. These thefts represent a serious handicap to the war effort. Always padlock your cycle and make a note of its description. Many machines that come into the hands of the police are not claimed because their owners cannot identify them". Vigilant backed this up with: "Be aware of the covetous eyes of unscrupulous people on your bicycles, people ready to appropriate them if they get the chance. (Vigilant may have been thinking of a report of a burglar, who grabbed the bicycle of an off-duty police officer, in order to make a quick get-away from the scene of his crime). Your machine is a valuable asset under present circumstances. Make a note of its number, which is usually under the saddle or at the foot of

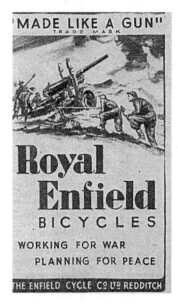

the back stay". As a child of five during the war, Yvonne Thornely recalls that her group of little friends, aged about seven and eight years old, thought it was great fun to hide the police constable's bicycle: "We would follow him about the village and when he went into somebody's house we would grab the bicycle and between us we would wheel it up the road and round the corner, out of sight". Publicity of the day backs up the shortage of bicycles; Phillips Cycles launched a series of adverts promoting spares and repair products, the only items they could supply in wartime. During the war the most common from of private transport was the bicycle and the ownership of a bike was every small boy's dream. Ivor, Yvonne's husband said that his father got him a bike from somewhere and gave him his first riding lessons in the roads near the family dairy. Ivor said he lost control of the bike and crashed over the wall and into the bushes surrounding the Clive Vale Police Station. The forks on the bike were twisted beyond repair, a disaster in wartime with the shortage of spares. But somehow his father found some replacement forks (better not to ask where, said Ivor.) The scheme to stop cycle thefts was soon called the "Mind my Bike Campaign", from the catchphrase of the

popular radio comedian, Jack Warner, who always used the words, "Mind my bike", to conclude his act.

Post war, Jack Warner went on to play Police Constable Dixon in the popular and long running BBC television series, Dixon of Dock Green. He portrayed the character of a firm but kindly policeman, in the manner of the constables still fondly remembered by the WWII generation.

Jack Warner in the role of PC Dixon of Dock Green

ACT SIX 1944

In January 1944, Chief of Police Cargill enlisted in the army and served on the staff of the Civil Affairs Organisation in France and Germany, with the rank of Lieutenant Colonel.

Lt. Col. Angus Gordon Cargill, B.E.M. Chief Constable of Hastings from April, 1942 to September, 1954.

A strange story of a deserter, headlined in the local paper as," Left Army and Went to Sea", was uncovered by Detective Sergeant Stanley Copper, who apprehended a man at Ore Village, just outside Hastings. (Stanley Copper lived at Ore; his house on The Ridge, close to the St Helens Police Station, was an emergency civil defence post during the war). The offender was charged with assuming a name other than that by which he was known. He was found to have been a deserter from the Royal Army Ordnance Corp since 1942, yet Supt Buddle stated in court that everything he could say about the man was in his favour. The deserter said that he had been called up before his 20th birthday but had got fed up with inactivity when he was home on leave, took his younger brother's identity card and got a job in a merchant seamen's club. After several attempts to get to sea, he got a place on a Polish steamer. Later, he obtained a seaman's identity card and joined a Dutch steamship, where he remained until he fell ill and was admitted to a sanatorium. Superintendent Buddle said that the man had been useful in the merchant navy on two ships, was now very sick but no doubt the military would do right by him. The "deserter" was remanded in custody to await military escort.

A 12 year old boy, described in court as bright but cunning and untruthful, by the Probation Officer, Mr. Hogan, had broken his recognisances, after having been bound over for two years. He had stolen 25/6d (£1.28) that his mother had given him to pay the butcher and he had also stolen sweet coupons from her and sold them to other boys. He said that this was out of revenge, as his mother had hit him. The father said he had used the strap on the boy but when the Clerk to the Magistrates, Colonel Langham, asked if he had also used the stick the father said no. The boy was sent to a remand home to await a vacancy in an approved school; at that time the nearest such establishments to Hastings were in Herstmonceux and Goudhurst. The first such institution, Borstal, gave its name to the entire system. The development of this new form of custody for young offenders came about slowly. In 1900 a small group of boys was carefully selected according to their likely ability to respond to specialized training. They were gathered in Bedford prison, to be taught a trade and to be helped to lead a new life, on discharge from prison. In 1902, a wing of the convict prison at Borstal at Richmond was taken over for a similar purpose. The boys were expected to work hard, and were given special

A Borstal institution

supervision on discharge, through the Borstal Association. A modified system was soon introduced in local prisons, under which young offenders were, as far as possible, separated from adult prisoners and given a little more attention than previously. Large numbers of Borstal trainees and prisoners were released at the outbreak of war and the premises were converted to other uses. From the autumn of 1940, however, the prison inmate numbers began to rise steadily. To ease overcrowding, one third remission was introduced as an emergency measure; and the use of open prisons for adults became accepted, when it was demonstrated that numbers of adult male prisoners could be trusted in open conditions. The numbers sentenced to Borstal training rose steeply and the inadequate number of places available in the institutions meant that many trainees had to spend a considerable period in a local prison, waiting for allocation to young offenders' institutions. The Criminal Justice Act abolished the Borstal system in 1982.

The inquiry by Colonel Langham, concerning the use of the strap and the stick as a domestic punishment in the case of the boy who stole the milk money, would not have been seen as inappropriate in 1944. The punishment of birching was still lawful and a sentence of corporal punishment could have been given to an older boy and it was also used as discipline in Borstal institutions. The device used for whippings was not a rod or cane but a bundle of birch twigs with a wire-like texture. Ex-Inspector Banks made reference to the punishment of birching: He said that in the thirties it could be carried out in the police station and sometimes the sons of police officers were given a warning, by being taken to see the "horse", to which the offender about to be given a birching was strapped. Ex-Inspector Banks acknowledged that such punishments are not acceptable today but added that boys who received a birching often admitted in later years that it had stopped them from following a life of crime. The old-time police officers talked about the summary justice meted out by the constables on the beat. They said that many youngsters who committed minor offences did not get to court. One ex-officer said: "We used to give them a clip round the ear and a good talking to and then they were taken home to their fathers, for more of the same". This system of rough justice extended to adults too, as this quote reveals: "I did my early policing in the Hastings and St Leonards area when Hollington was just wild country, with a few cottages here and there. Some local, gypsy

An Isle of Man police officer holding a birching rod

families camped there and fights often broke out between them. The police were called in to sort it out and we used to set about them with our batons, to quiet them down".

In March 1944, a fourteen year-old Hastings boy, described as having a military mind, stole a Sten gun, valued at £5, the property of the War Department. A Royal Army Service Corps driver had left the gun on a bed from where it disappeared. The boy admitted taking the gun and hiding it in an empty house. He used the gun in a game of soldiers and fired it with some old bullets he had found; he was the leader of a gang of boys that was fond of playing soldiers and commandos. Superintendent Buddle said the offence was serious and the boy should understand that dealing with firearms was very dangerous. He had not been under the notice of the police before so he was bound over for a year. In an additional juvenile court case in April 1944, it was stated that two boys broke into Home Guard premises and stole rifles, a revolver and ammunition. They ran away from home with two other boys and slept out on the Crowhurst Marshes all night. They returned home and hid the items under some wood and coal, stored in a shed. An older boy, a corporal in the youth organisation, the Air Training Corp, came to hear about the theft and he took control of the weapons and ammunition, fearing the boys might do some damage. He intended to return the stolen armaments, "After the hullabaloo had died down". The ATC youth was before the court on a charge of unlawfully receiving the stolen items. His solicitor, Mr. Morgan, asked the bench to treat it as a technical offence and the magistrates recorded a conviction but no penalty was imposed.

The wartime conditions on the home front offered endless opportunities to boys to exploit their mischievous tendencies, often

Hastings wartime Air Training Corp

with no grasp of the gravity of their actions. Two boys were apprehended and brought before the Juvenile Court for throwing rocks and pieces of wood into a static water tank. These huge, circular open-topped tanks were for the emergency use of the National Fire Service, should the normal supply of water fail during an air raid. Debris in the tanks could have restricted the flow of water through the firefighters' hoses. These tanks were often sited in pub car parks and there were a number of cases nationwide of drunks and adventurous children drowning in them. Surely the very youngest "criminals" during the war period in Hastings were two small boys, aged eight and six years, who went on a destructive rampage in July 1944, on properties along a stretch of Old London Road. They entered a solicitor's garden, reached inside the open window of his study and grabbed documents, which they scattered along the road. They then went into the garden of the Sacred Heart Convent and cut down one hundred bunches of grapes, valued at £18, and also pulled up beds of young onion plants.

They then turned their attention to the St Mary Star of the Sea Catholic Church, where they scattered votive candles around and set fire to tapestries and banners valued at £100. The older of the two boys, was described, when appearing in court as being: "Of innocent gaze, delicate looking and neatly dressed". The boy's mother, who was very distressed, said that the eight year-old had only given trouble in the past few months, since he had got in with a group of older lads. Clerk to the Magistrates, Colonel Langham, said to him, in kindly tones: "You are a naughty boy! Why do you do these things?" To which the child replied: "I don't know." The boy's mother promised to look after him better in future and he promised to be good. Both offenders were too young to be charged and the case was dismissed. The practice of the non-publication of the names of juvenile offenders caused Vigilant to comment: "I am certain that if the names of juvenile offenders were published there would be fewer children before the magistrates. Not only would publicity generate a wholesome sense of personal shame for bringing disgrace on the family, it would also prevent the anonymous culprits and their families from taking a light view of being brought to court".

Superintendent Buddle retired at the end of March 1944. He said: "After thirty years I have grown to love this town and the people in it. I have always striven to be a friend and helper to everyone here". Originally from Brighton, Mr. Buddle had been severely wounded on the Somme on July 1st 1916. He was invalided home but continued to serve as a Sergeant Instructor. For the last ten years of his service in the Hastings Force he was in charge of the police and juvenile courts. It was said that his scrupulous fairness was always noticeable. During WWII, Mr. Buddle showed himself to be efficient in handling numerous major incidents; he experienced some lucky escapes and had helped in rescuing and attending a number of people who were injured in air raids. Vigilant was fulsome in his praise of the retiring Superintendent Buddle: "His natural friendliness has earned him public affection and he will be remembered for his beneficent work, including that with the police-aided Boot and Clothing Fund. Mr. Buddle believed that repressive tactics would make the town unpopular with visitors and prospective residents and the Hastings Police had shown, over a long period, that discipline and order can be maintained without harsh or pettifogging measures". Various local institutions made recognition of the police career of Superintendent Buddle; the Watch Committee and Borough Magistrates presented him

1944. Lord Goschen, Commandant of the Sussex Constabulary, inspecting the Hastings Division of the Special Constabulary. Also shown Major E. H. Langham. T.D. Commandant of the Hastings Specials, and Superintendent W.J. Buddle

with a mahogany, knee-hole desk and a vellum booklet inscribed with the names of the 37 donors. Mr. Percy Idle, Clerk of the Peace said: "It is a great loss, some of us are sorry to see him go at such an early age and when manpower is so short". On the occasion of a subsequent civic tribute, Ex-Superintendent William Buddle's response made it clear that his retirement was not voluntary: "It was a great blow to me when I was told to retire; it was not my wish, at this most difficult time of the war, to be cut off from service, just as we were getting our toes on the road to victory". A measure of the affection in which he was held by his police colleagues is that his nickname was "Uncle Bill". The post of Police Superintendent was filled by Inspector George Knell.

It was announced in the first report from the newly amalgamated Sussex Police Force, presented by the Chief Constable Major. J Ferguson, that crime figures for the previous year had fallen. Also listed were the staff numbers for the Hastings Division of East Sussex: 1 Assistant Chief Constable, 1 Superintendent, 7 Inspectors, 3 Sub Inspectors, 17 Sergeants, 85 Constables and 1 Policewoman. The

1944

Police Auxiliaries comprised- 12 First Police Reserve, 32 Police War Reserve, 180 Special Constabulary and 10 Women Auxiliary Police Corp. There had been innovations in the police transport system; mobile receiving sets were fitted to 2 police cars and the fleet of four

Superintendent George Knell with Hastings Division Women's Auxiliary Police Corp

police cars and one van were fitted with loud hailers; the van was also equipped as an emergency police station. Ex-Inspector Banks brought his remarkable memory to bear on identifying the women police auxiliaries. He said that on the front, first right of the photograph is Joan Hammond, back row third from right is Mrs Dorothy Judge, (nee Ducue) who was a typist in the War Duties Section and she worked there with Vincent Batts, George Shepherd and Bob Tester. She did, however, have the opportunity to make one wartime arrest, of an errand boy who she spotted stealing some meat from another errand boy's basket. She also suffered the indignity, for a police officer, of being given a £2 fine for an infringement of the blackout regulations. Until he joined the military, Mrs Judge's husband, Leslie was an Inspector in the Police Specials and their son, Maxwell, became a police officer after the war. In the back row second right, Miss Burton,

120

a rally driver, who would drive for the police when required. Miss Mantell, seated in the front, second left was the police force photographer. Miss Mantell sometimes drove for Mr Cargill. They were returning to Hastings from police business on July 19th 1943, via East Grinstead, just after the town had suffered the second worst air

The wrecked Whitehall Cinema, East Grinstead

raid disaster in Sussex. It was a dull Friday afternoon in the school holidays and the town's Whitehall Cinema was packed. A bomb exploded in the auditorium and the walls, dome and girders collapsed onto the audience, killing entire families. The final death toll was over a hundred. Miss Mantell had her camera with her and took a series of pictures at the scene that helped in identifying the dead.

The reinstatement of banned area status for Hastings and St Leonards came into force from 1st April 1944; local hotels and guest houses suffered Easter cancellations and the prevailing uncertainty affected summer bookings. One banned area offender, who was caught in the renewed purge on illegal visitors, was a man who said that his presence in Hastings was unintentional. He said he suffered from sleepiness, after a blow on the head some time previously and he had inadvertently fallen asleep on the train. He added that his wife, who had left him in December 1943, had thrown his identity card away. Police Superintendent Knell said that although the man lived in South London he had been wandering about the country and had already

The police inspect travellers' documents
at Hastings Railway Station

been apprehended by the police in Eastbourne for failing to produce his identity card. The offender was charged with being in a protected area without permission and failing to produce an identity card. He was sent to prison for one month and told that the doctor at Lewes prison would look into his mental condition. Vigilant took this opportunity to remind the people of Hastings and St Leonards what a great amount of military and police time was wasted by citizens who fail to sign and carry their identity cards: "Carrying one's identity card must be as habitual as carrying a handkerchief." His remark may have been viewed cynically by his readers; handkerchiefs, when available in the shops, required clothing coupons and many people had reached the stage of making do with scraps of torn sheeting and rags. By this point in the war shortages of all kinds were an every day matter and many people were prepared to take extraordinary risks to obtain a few extra rations. Stella Francis worked at a country grocery

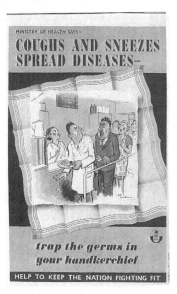

shop, combined with post office, just outside Hastings. She remembered when a flying bomb fell near the shop and the windows shattered. Everything in the shop was covered with debris and broken glass. The stock of butter and cheese, which in those days was delivered in blocks, had been penetrated with splinters of glass. Stella said: "The Ministry of Food Inspector came out to the shop at once, to impound the damaged stock. This was to prevent it making its way onto the black market. Although the butter and cheese, full of bits of glass posed a potential danger, people would stop at nothing to get a little extra food".

It was inevitable with so many weapons being in the possession of partially-trained civilians that accidents would occur: A woman at Battle was killed when her lodger, an agricultural engineer and a private in the Home Guard, was demonstrating how to load a Sten gun. After a Sunday, Home Guard parade he had loaned his rifle to a HG corporal, who wanted to go to the rifle range in the coming week. In exchange, the private took home the corporal's Sten gun, plus four loaded magazines. When the Home Guard got back to his lodgings, his landlady was curious about how the gun operated and persuaded the man to load it. He held the loaded gun against his right thigh pointing away from the woman, who he warned not to touch the trigger but the gun may have caught on his clothing and it discharged, the bullet entering the woman's thigh. She was bleeding profusely and a doctor and an ambulance were sent for but the woman was declared dead on arrival at the hospital. The coroner asked the Home Guard if no one had told him never to demonstrate firearms of any kind and he replied: "I am afraid not but I have been handling guns ever since I remember".

Sten guns – "the plumber's nightmare"

The victim's cousin said that the dead woman was very interested in how everything worked and would have been persistent in her request to see the gun loaded. The Sten gun was not popular among troops, who called it the "Plumber's Nightmare", a reference to its resemblance to a piece of tubing and ungainly design. In addition to jamming, the gun was also very subject to unexpectedly discharging, especially if dropped, which resulted in many accidental deaths.

The wartime ex-police officers interviewed for this book preferred to talk about routine work or amusing anecdotes rather than dwell on the horrors they witnessed. The only comment volunteered by one ex-officer of the scenes he encountered during post bombing rescue work was: "It was pretty gruesome". Some idea of how appalling it must have been can be gathered from this account taken from the Hastings Local History Group publication, Hastings Bygones, Edition 4: Helen Roodt, aged 70 wrote: "During the war I lived in Caves Road, in a three-story house that overlooked Towner's furniture store warehouse, which was used as a mortuary for the bodies from bombing raids. The bodies were brought into the yard in Hastings Corporation dust carts, with the blood running from them. Body parts were placed on tarpaulins in the yard and hosed down, in preparation for identification. If not identified, the remains went for communal burial. My family was moved away, to a house over the road because my mum used to stand at the window overlooking Towner's yard".

Following the D-Day Invasion of Europe, the ban on health and leisure visits to Hastings was lifted by the War Office on 25th August 1944. The beach was re-opened shortly afterwards and it was announced that from 17th September a form of half lighting would be permitted, under a dim-out, thus doing away with the total blackout regulation that had kept the police, air raid wardens and the magistrates courts busy for five years. At least six Hastings families, who returned home after spending the war years elsewhere, were dismayed to find that their homes had been looted of their entire contents; others found that all their bedding was stolen, with no hope of ever bringing the culprits to justice. The Citizens Advice Bureau and the Central Aid Council gave what help they could but returnees also had to cope with a shortage of houses to rent and increased rents for those that were available; other houses were for sale only. The official advice to some families was to stay away.

1944

Mr. Harold Glenister appeared before the Hastings Licensing Magistrates to make application on behalf of licensees for an extension to trading hours for the Christmas period. The presiding magistrate, Mr. Heron, questioned the need for an extension in the face of shortage of supplies of alcohol and he added that Christmas was a time to be at home. He also raised the matter of the lack of public transport; the bus service ceased to run at 9.00pm. Mr. Glenister said that 10.00pm was too early for pubs and similar premises to close during the Christmas holiday. Also the lack of supplies of alcohol was in part a myth and the attitude of licensees on the matter of shortages was, if supplies ran out- too bad! As for transport, most customers were locals and travelling was not a consideration. For the police, Superintendent Knell said there was no objection and the extension was granted. Three soldiers on leave, in anticipation of the seasonal festivities and to celebrate their return from the war front, over-indulged to such a degree that they were arrested for being drunk and incapable, on a bus at Silverhill. They spent the night in police custody and when they appeared before the magistrate in the morning they apologized, saying that it was so long since they had had alcohol it went straight to their heads. The magistrate, in congenial mood, imposed no sentence and said: "You have already wasted one day of your leave, you can go now and I wish you all a Happy Christmas".

ACT SEVEN 1945

During WWII, the notions of personal choice and ambition in work and career were often set aside, as the nation worked for one aim: victory. That is not to say that people were unconcerned with personal advancement and many owed their subsequent success in civilian life to training and experience gained in war service. Under the National Service Act, thousands of civilians signed up for essential war work and became stuck in arduous, dead-end jobs, from which they could not easily extricate themselves. Those who did not follow the letter of the law when they tried to leave a job could find themselves in court. Three women, all over the age of forty, appeared before Hastings

Magistrates, charged with leaving their work without the permission of the National Service Officer. They had formerly been running a boarding house in the town but the war had brought this venture to an end. They put their furniture in a Hastings repository but because they could not keep up the storage fees they had to forfeit their goods. In February 1941 all three volunteered for National Service Employment and were sent to work in the London North East Railway goods yard, at King's Cross. They were given jobs as porters (at that time 1,700 women were employed by the company) doing heavy work of the kind usually carried out by men, shifting goods from the railway wagons and loading them onto vans. They were regarded by their boss as satisfactory employees. Later their home in London was bomb-damaged and it became damp, making worse the rheumatism from which one of the women suffered. They made an application to leave their jobs but on receiving no reply, they left London and returned to Hastings in September 1944, to wait confirmation of release from employment, unaware that they were breaking the law. The magistrate, Alderman Blackman said that the defendants now understood they had committed an offence but the prosecution had agreed to be kind and lenient with them and there would be no penalty, under the Probation of Offenders Act. In another case of wrongfully leaving National Service Employment the local paper ran a punning headline; "Busman Got a Place in the Sun!" The man had left his job with the London Transport Passenger Board, without the permission of the National Service Officer. He had made three applications and two appeals for his discharge but they were all refused, after a full investigation. In court the defendant explained that after his wife died he found his household expenses too much to cope with; he also considered that after the war a bus driver of his age, 51, would not be of much use to his employer. He was in search of some security when he found he could become the licensee of the Sun Inn at Hastings and he thought it would be a good proposition. The London Passenger Transport Board was willing to take him back as there was a shortage of staff and he was such a good driver. The defendant was fined £5 but there was no mention of whether he ever took up his post behind the bar of the Sun Inn.

The Hastings Brewster Sessions, the meeting of the licensing magistrates, held annually in the first two weeks of February was thrown into confusion in 1945, by the surprise announcement of the intended and immediate resignation from the Licensing Bench, of its chairman, Magistrate E T Heron. His resignation was a protest at having been asked to submit a draft of his speech to the licensees, for the prior approval of his fellow magistrates and at less than 24 hours' notice. He said that he refused to have his speech discussed and censored, under the inference that he could not be trusted to make suitable remarks. He added to the drama by saying: "I shall therefore immediately leave this seat and this session and I hope that proceedings will go on as normal". Vigilant seized upon this drama in high places. He first paid tribute to Mr. Heron's "broad minded and valuable work", as a Licensing Justice and continued: "If the Brewster Sessions have recently been criticized for being out of date, any taint of dullness was removed by the action of Mr. Heron at their meeting this week. I feel that the committee was justified in asking to see the chairman's speech, as the public assumes that it is the opinion of every member". The Brewster Sessions moved through its agenda in spite of the excitement and in his report on behalf of Hastings Police Force, Superintendent Knell drew attention to complaints he had received about the annoyance caused by the continuous singing and piano playing in some public houses. He said: "I have warned three particular licensees and have asked them to stop it". Vigilant, a lover of classical music had plenty to say on this topic too: "I have commented previously on the curious fact that in this country, music and alcoholic refreshment often lead to disharmony, and not solely in the musical sense. Hours of maudlin wailing take place in some public houses, to the distress of the licensee and his customers, who would gladly accept a ban on spontaneous vocalism; music can inflame as many breasts as it soothes. In these days of endless radio crooners, people can do without this noise when they drop in for a friendly glass". It seems that there been fewer locals, "dropping in for a friendly glass". According to Superintendent Knell's report, 1944 had seen only 8 persons convicted for drunkenness and all were non-residents. He said it was a reflection of the hard times being endured that few people could afford over-indulgence in alcohol.

Spring 1945 brought an almost end of term feeling in the town's public affairs: The Town Council held the final meeting at its wartime quarters in Summerfields on 10th April 1945. One of the subjects under discussion was the immediate derequisitioning of Hastings hotels and boarding houses, in cases where the owners wished to regain possession of their properties and re-open their businesses. The

Holiday-makers contemplate happier times ahead

Town Council heard the annual report from The Sussex Chief of Police, Lieutenant Colonel Ferguson. He commended the conduct of the Hastings Division of the Sussex Police Force: "They have carried out their work in the best traditions of the police force and at no time was it more noticeable than during the flying bomb attacks, when the strain became acute. There were constant calls on all ranks, day and night but they were never found wanting and the Specials were there to lend a hand. Notwithstanding the long hours, arduous training and duties, the conduct of the division has been excellent. Members of the Hastings Force have been commended by the justices and myself, for their intelligence and ability in handling various matters". In a later statement to the press, Police Superintendent George Knell, on behalf of the Hastings Police Force, expressed his admiration and sincere thanks to the townspeople for the magnificent manner in which they stood up to five years of war. At the outbreak of war there were six Army Reservists in the Police Force and these were called to service in 1939. Other police officers served in the forces and all returned safely, except Police Constable Roy Baker, who joined the Royal Air Force. He became a Pilot Officer/Observer and was killed with all his crew over France.

On the 7th May, the Admiralty announced that lighting restrictions were lifted in the coastal areas, as they were no longer necessary for defence purposes. As it was becoming clear that the announcement of victory was imminent, preparation for commemorative and celebratory events were laid; church services, military and civil processions and street parties were planned and it was presumed that Hastings and St Leonards' licensed premises would be well patronised. On behalf of the local Licensed Victuallers Association, Mr. H Glenister applied for an hour's extension to public house opening times. The Clerk of the Court, Colonel Langham, pointed out that the application related to a

A victory street party in Hardwicke Road, Hastings

day as yet unknown but Mr. Glenister said that he did not recollect anything in law which prohibited the magistrates from granting an extension for an unknown date and the application was granted. On the 8th May 1945, at 4.00pm, shortly after Winston Churchill's speech to the nation, declaring victory and the end of hostilities in Europe, the Mayor appeared on Hastings Town Hall balcony, to be greeted by a huge crowd and enthusiastic applause. Ex-Inspector Banks spoke of the victory celebrations as causing no trouble to the police. "I recollect much church bell-ringing, parades and a great many street parties but everything took place in a very orderly manner". The police choir performed in Alexandra Park. The choir master was Mr H Vincent Batts, who was serving in the Police War Reserve. The choir had an audition with Leslie Woodgate, the choral conductor for the BBC and gave two broadcast performances. Even during the celebrations there

1945. Hastings Police Choir giving one of their many performances in the Alexandra Park, Hastings.
Conductor:- Mr. H. Nincent Batts, L.R.A.M. F.R.C.O.

were still those who were just as willing to take advantage of the newly declared victory as they were to exploit war conditions: On VE-Day there was a theft from the Wheatsheaf Pub at Bohemia Road. The thief, who it was believed entered the pub via a ground floor window left partly open, stole 200 cigarettes, a bottle of brandy and £30-40 in notes and £9 in coins, which were in a tankard, hidden in one of the bars. There is no record of anyone being charged with the offence.

The people of Hastings and St Leonards had endured 85 enemy air attacks of various kinds and numerous tip and run raids from 1940 to 1944. A total of 550 high explosive bombs, 14 small bombs of a special type and 27 unexploded bombs, twelve oil incendiary bombs, about 750 incendiaries and 15 flying bombs fell on the town. During these attacks 154 people were killed, 260 were injured and detained in hospital and 439 were slightly injured. The town's housing stock was badly affected with 436 houses and other buildings destroyed and 14, 818 properties damaged. Hastings and St Leonards put its strength behind every aspect of the war effort. The town's sons and daughters left home, many for the first time, to join H M Services or National Service Schemes; many gave their lives. Hastings and St Leonards, not a rich community by any means, collected millions of pounds during special war fund raising campaigns; Wings for Victory Week, Salute the Soldier Week, War Weapons Week and Spitfire Week. On two separate occasions, the town raised enough cash to buy a destroyer and a Spitfire. Residents also saved hundreds of thousands of pounds via the National Savings Scheme as well as contributing enthusiastically to salvage drives and adapting with stoicism to the day-to-day drudgery of doing without and the countless restrictions imposed upon them. The most common remark made by today's senior citizens on this aspect of the war was: "We just got on with it".

For his first peacetime Flotsam and Jetsam column, Vigilant featured the town's current aggravation: "People who stayed put in Hastings during the war have no reason to be proud, arrogant or hostile to those who have returned to the town or have arrived as new residents. It is true that some people spent the war in comparative comfort, just by chance but others, who were sent away, also suffered hardships. Let us have no more comparisons from the thoughtless minority, who indulge in mischief making. Stamp it out!" Frederick Goodsell -"Vigilant"- continued as editor to the Hastings and St Leonards Observer until 1965, when he retired due to the onset of an illness, described as a nervous breakdown. He died in April 1972, at the age of 63.

Mr. W H Dyer, nephew of Sir Alfred Dyer, former editor of the Observer, wrote a tribute to "Freddie": " He was a man of culture who could make written words live...he maintained the strength of the Observer's influence on local thought and helped to support residents' morale in wartime... His leading articles were often referred to in the town as brilliant... Even in later years, when illness had left its mark on him, he never lost his grasp of current affairs or his capacity for gentle raillery". Although Frederick Goodsell was well known as the editor as the local newspaper, for his involvement in his church, his love of music and playing the piano and painting water colours, almost nothing seems to be remembered of his private life; few seemed to have known him personally. An Observer cub reporter, now in his nineties, recalled that Goodsell lived with his mother and never married. Tantalizingly, a card attached to one of his funeral floral tributes was signed, "Friend and Colleague-Madam S". Viewed from today's perspective, Vigilant's wartime articles may seem misogynistic, pompous and hectoring but he has left an interesting account of the morals and foibles of a small, seaside town under fire. He was also instrumental, in April 1945, in compiling and publishing the book, called "Hastings and St Leonards in the Front Line", a collection of photographs and reports of the enemy destruction of the town. The book remains a valuable resource to all who are interested in local, World War Two home front history.

After Hitler was defeated it came to light that one of the locations chosen for the landing of a German invasion was Hastings' flat, accessible beaches and its townspeople would have been among the first to feel the effects of enemy rule. If anyone ever had any doubts about the harsh regime Hitler had in mind for the occupation of Great Britain these were dispelled by the post-victory discovery of a German secret document called, "The Military Administration of England", (the German idiom for Great Britain). The document was a plan to transform Britain into Germany's war workshop, following the invasion that Hitler had planned to take place in September 1940. This summary of the document is taken from The War Illustrated, September 1945: "Britain was to become the producer of weapons, under Nazi direction, for Hitler's battle against Russia. Under the plan, as soon as the country was defeated, all male Britons aged 17 to 45 were to be deported to Europe, possibly for use as slave labourers; German workers would be sent to Britain to replace them. The remaining population would work and live under a military regime:

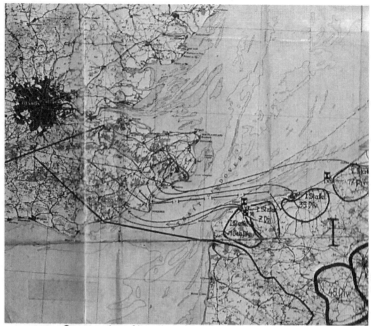

German plan of invasion of Britain's South East coast.

Any person impeding the German war effort by guerilla activities was to be shot; hostages would have been taken as a security measure against this. National laws already in force would only have been maintained if they were not contrary to the German occupation. The country's state of health was only significant if it threatened national resources. A limited fraternization policy for the troops was to be allowed but only insofar as it did not jeopardize military security. German soldiers were to be allowed to buy anything they wished but instead of payment they could issue certificates to the value of the purchase. Germany currency was to be imposed and all public utilities; gas, electricity, railways, public monuments and works of art were to be under the special protection of the army. Industrial concerns and commercial firms and banks were to be kept open; closing them without adequate reason would be severely punished. Agricultural and industrial products of all kind were to be requisitioned; this included fuel, rubber, leather, timber, textiles, ore and semi-precious stones. Farmers and dealers would only be allowed to provide products in quantities to meet the most urgent needs of indigenous consumers.

The concealment of firearms, including shot guns and other hunting arms was to be punishable by death. Severe punishment would be passed by military courts on those civilians who associated with prisoners of war, indulged in subversive activities or insulted the German Army of Occupation or its commanders. Listening to non-German radio broadcasts, except those permitted by the occupying forces, would become a punishable offence; owning a radio transmitter would have incurred a death sentence. A sunset to sunrise curfew was to be imposed. The document revealed intricate arrangements for the economic enslavement of the British people. A military, economic staff was to function under the Commander-in-Chief of the German Army. This staff was to be installed in all harbours and industrial centres and would be in charge of transporting raw materials and completed war equipment. German administrative experts were to join the army of occupation, to mastermind agriculture and industrial production and the distribution of food". One might say that by the end of the war many of the regulations that the Germans planned to introduce were already in force in Great Britain: The death penalty for spying, compulsory national service, strict government controls over every aspect of life as well as rationing of many commodities and severe shortages of others and the setting of curfews and restriction of movement. However, self imposed state controls differ entirely from those of an occupying power and there is no doubt that certain sections of British society would have been dealt with as cruelly as they had been in countries occupied by the Nazis.

When Ex-Constable Ken Buddle took up his duties in 1946, Hastings was far from recovered from the effects of war; although the majority of the bomb sites had been cleared, almost no work had started on re-building. Of his superiors he said. "In my time, most of the police sergeants had served either in World War Two or the previous war and their military training taught them how to manage men and exert discipline in a way that was firm but fair; they were good old sergeants". Ken Buddle's police post war duties followed a routine already set by generations of police officers; that of patrolling the beat and thus gaining a detailed knowledge of local residents and properties. He said that when he was on duty outside Ore Village School the home-going children would greet him by name. When asked about the police aided boot and clothing fund Ken said that it was still in operation during his early days with the police force, officers would take note of any child who seemed in need of footwear and pass the name to the administrators of the fund.

After the war, the Town Hall Magistrates' Court became inadequate for its purpose. Present day magistrate, Michael Chaloner, served his first few years on the Bench in the Town Hall Court in the early 1970s. He said: "When the court schedule was particularly busy, the upstairs council chamber and other rooms were pressed into service. The main council chamber, which overlooks busy Queens Road, was quite unsuitable; passing traffic often made it almost impossible to hear those who were softly spoken. To retire to consider their verdict, the Bench was obliged to walk past the witnesses and the accused, which was sometimes intimidating. Other inadequate sized rooms, such as the robing room and juvenile court room were used for court hearings. The move to larger premises was long overdue". There was no distinct cut-off point between the use of the old court premises and the new. (The Town Hall Central Police Station had moved to 4-5 Robertson Terrace in the mid-1950s). Jean Gill said that the law offices, including the fines department, of which she eventually became senior finance officer, moved to the Bohemia Road premises quite some time prior to the opening of the new court and much time was lost daily, running between the two sites.

At the end of December 1971 the last Quarter Sessions was held in Hastings; from that date cases were sent to trial at the new Crown Court, which replaced Assizes and Quarter Sessions. All of the officers of the court would continue to function elsewhere, except for Mr F G Beckett, the Clerk of the Peace, an office which he had held for 20 years. Mr J Mainwaring Baines noted in his book, Historic Hastings: "The first mention of Quarter Sessions is in the White Book of the Cinque Ports when, at a Brotheryeld in 1594, an order was made that 'every town and member is to keep Quarter Sessions according to the King's dite'". The last voice to be heard in Hastings Quarter Sessions was that of Mr Fred Tough, the Jury Bailiff, when he gave the "cry" after the sitting: "Oyez! Oyez! Oyez! The business of this Quarter Sessions of the Peace is ended. All persons may depart herefrom. God Save the Queen!"

The new law court, built with an adjoining police station, on the site of

Summerfields School, Bohemia Road, began operating in early June 1975. The official opening of the court on 10th October was accompanied by strict security, of a kind previously unseen in Hastings. Every car was checked as it drove into the car park; police searched vehicle boots and interiors and their undersides were inspected with mirrors on rods. There were also armed police officers

Hastings and St Leonards Police Station

on the court roof. It should be remembered that this period was the height of the IRA attacks in the UK. As people entered the building, prior to the formal court opening, their names were checked on an official guest list. Invitations had to be shown and some people were "frisked". One member of the court staff recalled that the seating plan for guests turned into a diplomatic nightmare, as the protocol shifted with the random influx of important and unexpected arrivals.

The new courts, which had cost £710,000 to build, were declared open by the Lord Chief Justice, Lord Widgery, who had been the Recorder of Hastings from 1959 to 1961. In his opening address Lord Widgery hinted at forthcoming new legislation which would reduce the number

Hastings new law court at Summerfields

of people in prison on remand: "People are often remanded in custody because they have no fixed abode or it is feared they will not come back to court to answer their case. Sometimes it would be a good thing if they did not come back." He gave as an example a man who steals a bottle of milk in order to get a night's prison accommodation, which costs the taxpayer £40 per night. Lord Widgery considered that a magistrate should let him go: "So that he might try somewhere else. The ones to worry about are those liable to commit serious offences on bail or try to influence witnesses, these are cases where bail should not be granted". He went on to express his admiration of the work of magistrates, who deal with 98% of criminal cases. He added that it was important to have proper tools for the job, as represented by the fine new building at Summerfields. Lord Widgery, accompanied by the Chairman of the East Sussex Magistrates Committee, Mr G Parks, unveiled a commemorative plaque in the vestibule of the court building.

In 1976, a year after the closure of the old courtroom and to prepare it for use as an exhibition centre for the Hastings Embroidery, the council decided to remove the old oak panelling. A number of contractors put in tenders and the job went to Perkins Plant Hire Ltd, who was taken on to remove not only the panelling but the oak screen and benches. For all this 'salvage' Perkins paid the council £60. Councillor Eric Duck was outraged and said that the removal of the panelling was vandalism in its worst form and the whole thing was done too quickly. The Finance Committee Chairman responded by saying that he did not know what all the fuss was about, the panels had no historical or antique value and anyhow, there was dampness behind them. The collection of hand painted shields, which were installed in the Town Hall Magistrates' Courts in 1929, was saved and they now hang over the stairwell in the Bohemia Road Law Courts.

The three new Bohemia Road Magistrate Courtrooms are of an imposing design; lofty, stark and intimidating. The only decoration is the Royal Coat of Arms, set on the wall behind the bench, on which sit the three magistrates, raised almost 2 metres above the well of the court. This elevated position lends yet more gravitas to the proceedings, as does the long-established custom of those present rising to their feet when the magistrates enter or leave the court, and the bow that must directed to the bench on exiting the court in session. A few hours of watching a magistrate's court in the act of dispensing justice provided examples of cases that were a sharp contrast to those seen in the 1940s. Before the magistrates during one morning in 2004 were offences such as state benefit fraud, drug dealing and abuse and serious public violence whilst drunk.

In one case, a man of 19 was in the dock; he was a repeat offender, who had stolen cigarettes and a bottle of whisky, whilst drunk, from a late night store. He was unemployed and receiving a state benefit of £40 per week. He was sentenced to a Community Rehabilitation Order, obliging him to see his Probation Officer for one hour every week, to discuss job prospects. On hearing the sentence the defendant conducted a muttered conversation with his solicitor, who then told the bench that his client objected to the sentence, "Because it was an infringement of his personal liberty." The Chairman of the Bench remained implacable and said: "That is the sentence". This case immediately brought to mind Private Harry Henham, also aged 19, laid to rest in the Heroes' Corner of Hastings Cemetery in 1940. At Dunkirk he gave not just one hour, but his life, to preserve the freedom of his country.

Heraldic Shields from the Hastings Town Hall
Magistrates Court

APPENDIX

POLICE FORCE STAFF NUMBERS AND TRANSPORT FACILITIES IN 1854

In 1854 Hastings Police Force consisted of:

1 Inspector.

3 Sergeants.

9 Constables.

No official transport. A horse and cart/carriage was available as needed.

1854. Force members outside the original Police Station (later a Museum), in the High Street, Hastings.

THE HASTINGS DIVISION OF EAST SUSSEX POLICE STAFF NUMBERS AND TRANSPORT FACILITIES FOR 1944:

1 Assistant Chief Constable,

1 Superintendent,

7 Inspectors, 3 Sub Inspectors,

17 Sergeants,

85 Constables,

1 Policewoman.

The Police Auxiliaries comprised-

12 First Police Reserve,

32 Police War Reserve,

180 Special Constabulary

10 Female Auxiliary Police Corp.

Innovations to police transport system in 1944; mobile receiving sets were fitted to 2 police cars and the fleet of four police cars and its one van were fitted with loud hailers; the van was also equipped as an emergency police station.

1944. Lord Goschen, Commandant of the Sussex Constabulary, inspecting the Hastings Division of the Special Constabulary. Also shown Major E. H. Langham. T.D. Commandant of the Hastings Specials, and Superintendent W.J. Buddle

STAFF NUMBERS, TRANSPORT AND OTHER FACILITIES FOR THE SUSSEX POLICING DIVISION OF HASTINGS AND ROTHER 2004.

284 Police Officers comprising:
1 Chief Superintendent,
1 Superintendent,
3 Chief Inspectors,
14 Inspectors,
36 Sergeants,
234 Constables.
There are 109 members of Police Staff covering roles such as:
Police Community Support Officers,
Police Neighbourhood Support Officers,
Investigative Support Assistants,
Tape Summarisers.
Exhibits Clerks.

APPENDIX

Intelligence Analysts &Researchers.
Coroner's Officers.
Caretakers.
Administration Staff.
Crime Prevention Officers.

PC Clare Denny and PC Matthew Pearmain. Police officers with the Sussex
Policing Division of Hastings and Rother

APPENDIX

Reflecting the changed nature and hazards of contemporary crime and policing, the 21st century police officer wears personal armour and carries an incapacitation spray. They are equipped with a baton, handcuffs, radio, notebook and a first aid kit that includes rubber gloves and a face mask.

VEHICLES.

There are 39 patrol cars in the Neighbourhood Police Teams, which are, in the main, Ford Focus 1.8 diesel estates. These vehicles have high visibility markings with blue strobe-light roof bars, headlamp flashers and wailer sirens to maximise their presence when answering emergency calls. There are also 14 unmarked vehicles for detective use and 4 Mercedes-Benz Sprinter diesel Police Support Unit vehicles. These are used primarily by the Local Support Team and are marked high visibility vehicles with blue lights and wailer sirens that transport specialist-trained uniformed officers, to support their regular neighbourhood police team colleagues.

Also in use are two mobile close circuit television (CCTV) Ford Transit-based vehicles, which are high visibility marked, one of these vehicles has mobile police station capability the other has a custodial area, where prisoners can be detained en-route to the cell block at Hastings.

There are two lightweight 125cc trials motorcycles, primarily for off-road use and the Roads Policing Unit (formerly Traffic Branch), based at Bexhill, which covers the eastern end of the county, including Hastings. There are 2 high powered BMW bikes which are liveried with blue lights and sirens and deal with emergency response, particularly road traffic accidents.

The helicopter, known internally as Hotel 900 as its call sign is H900, is based at Shoreham Airport, though is often deployed over and above Hastings. H900 provides invaluable support to officers on the ground and

At least 1 dog unit is on duty around the clock and the officers concerned with dogs use high visibility marked Vauxhall Zafira people carriers, which have specially converted air-conditioned rear compartments where the canine officer can be safely and comfortably transported from job to job.

COULD YOU BE A MAGISTRATE?
In present times, magistrates are selected from members of the local community and from all walks of life. No formal qualifications are required but magistrates must have the attributes of intelligence, common sense, integrity and the capacity to act fairly. All magistrates are carefully trained before sitting and continue to receive training throughout their service, particularly in the first two years following appointment. They are unpaid volunteers but may receive allowances to cover travelling expenses and subsistence.

Magistrates deal with two categories of crime. Serious, referred to as either-way offences, e.g. theft, fraud, where magistrates may deal with the case or refer it to the Crown Court. Less Serious, referred to as summary offences, e.g. traffic matters, which are only dealt with by magistrates. The maximum penalty available to magistrates is six months' imprisonment but magistrates can impose community penalties, compensation and fines.

The Lord Chancellor requires that each bench should broadly reflect the community it serves in terms of gender, ethnic origin, geographical spread, occupation and political affiliation. Achieving a balance is, however, a secondary consideration to the essential and pre-eminent requirement that a candidate must be personally suitable for appointment, possessing the qualities required in a magistrate. Since 1997, the retirement age for magistrates is 70. The Lord Chancellor will not generally appoint a candidate under the age of 27 or over the age of 65.

Each bench should have a roughly equal number of men and women. There should be sufficient magistrates of each sex who are eligible to sit in the family proceedings and youth courts, which must be made up of three magistrates and include a man and a woman, unless this is impractical. Advisory committees are making strenuous efforts to recruit suitable candidates from the ethnic minorities. The committees should also ensure that there are not too many magistrates on any one bench from the same village, neighbourhood or street. No more than 15% of the magistrates on a bench should be from the same occupational group. The political views of a candidate are not relevant to appointment. However, in the interests of balance, it is essential that the voting pattern for the area, as evidenced by the last two general elections, should be broadly reflected in the composition of the bench.

It is important that there are not too many magistrates on the bench from the same clubs or organisations. Candidates for the magistracy are specifically asked on the new application form if they are freemasons and if they are recommended for appointment they will be required to inform the chairman of the bench or the clerk to the justices if they subsequently become a freemason. Magistrates must have personal integrity and the ability to weigh evidence and reach reasoned decisions. They are required to live or work in the area and have good local knowledge and understanding of the local community. Magistrates must be able to work as a member of a team and be firm yet compassionate.

Almost anyone can apply to become a magistrate but the following will not be appointed: Anyone who is not of good character and personal standing: An un-discharged bankrupt, a serving member of Her Majesty's Forces, a member of a police force, a traffic warden or persons following any other occupation which might be seen to conflict with the role of a magistrate. Also not appointed are close relatives of a person who is already a magistrate on the same bench or anyone who, because of a disability, cannot carry out all the duties of a magistrate.

Court business takes place during working hours so there is a need to ask for employers to give staff time from work to fulfill this valuable task. There can be significant benefits to both employer and to employee; the magistrate-employee will have new learning opportunities and a focus beyond work that will bring benefits back into the workplace. Induction and basic training enhance and refine skills that are transferable to the world of work including: decision making skills, teamwork, communication skills, knowledge of different cultures and recognition of discrimination and acceptance of responsibility. Many supportive employers allow magistrates leave for these public duties in addition to their normal holiday entitlement. Many businesses give leave for court duties without loss of pay. However, where this is not possible, a basic loss of earnings allowance may be available. Training is almost always undertaken in the magistrates' own free time in the evenings and at weekends.

As magistrates become more experienced, they may be selected to undertake training for chairmanship which incorporates further skills in presentation, leadership and chairmanship and bringing out the best in people and empowering others in a team. Each magistrate is expected to undertake a fair share of the work of the bench. The Lord Chancellor requires that a magistrate should sit for at least 26 half days each year and up to 35 half days each year. In practice, most magistrates are in court for the equivalent of 18 days per year. Magistrates should be prepared to sit for a whole day if necessary. Magistrates normally exercise their duties as part of a bench of three. At all times they have available to them the advice of a qualified court clerk.

Over 95% of all criminal cases are dealt with by magistrates, either in the adult court, or in the youth court. The work involves, amongst other things, deciding on applications for bail, whether a defendant is guilty or not and passing sentences as appropriate. For a single criminal offence, committed by an adult, magistrates' sentencing powers include the imposition of fines, community service orders, probation orders or a period of not more than six months in custody. Magistrates may also sit in the Crown Court with a judge, to hear appeals from magistrates' courts against conviction or sentence and proceedings on committal to the Crown Court for sentence.

Magistrates decide many civil matters, particularly in relation to family work. Specially selected and trained members of the family court panels deal with a wide range of matters, most of which arise from the breakdown of marriage e.g. making orders for the residence of and contact with children. Proceedings relating to the care and control of children are also dealt with in family proceedings courts.

Members of specialist committees are responsible for the administration of the liquor licensing system and for the grant or refusal of applications for licenses and permits relating to betting and the registration of gaming clubs. Most magistrates carry out some routine licensing work. The civil jurisdiction also involves the enforcement of financial penalties and orders such as those in respect of non-payment of council tax. Magistrates are expected to play a part in the life of the bench and where possible, attend bench meetings etc. They may undertake work out of court, as members of committees. They are also expected to deal, at home, with requests for warrants for arrest and search and to take declarations of various kinds.

On reaching the age of 70, a magistrates' name is transferred to the supplemental list, unless they are the chairman of the bench, in which case they are entitled to remain in the active list until the end of the calendar year in which they attained their seventieth birthday. Magistrates will be sent a valedictory letter by the Lord Chancellor with a note explaining the duties which they may and may not perform while on the supplemental list. Magistrates who have served for 15 years or more may apply to have their names entered on the list. The Lord Chancellor may grant this application on the recommendation of the local advisory committee. When on the supplemental list a magistrate can: Sign any document for the purpose of authenticating another person's signature, take and authenticate by his/her signature any written declaration not made on oath. Magistrates can also give a certificate of facts within his/her knowledge or of his/her opinion as to any matter. In special circumstances and on a personal basis, former magistrates can be authorised by the Lord Chancellor to sit in the Crown Court for a specified period but powers are limited.

If you are interested in becoming a magistrate , application forms and information on the selection process are available from the secretary of your local advisory committee, whose name and address can be obtained from the office of the Clerk to the Justices in your local magistrates' court, or from the office of the Lay Magistracy Branch in London:
Lay Magistracy Branch
District Bench and Magistracy Division
Judicial Group
1st Floor
Selborne House

APPENDIX

54 Victoria Street, London SW1E 6QWTel: 020 7210 8990
Email:laymagistrates.judicialgroup@dca.gsi.gov.uk

BIBLIOGRAPHY

A History of the County Borough of Hastings Police. 1836-1967. Researched and written by Ex-Inspector Charles Banks. Out of print.

Gentlemen at War. 1939-1945 by Roy Ingleton. Published by Cranborne publications.

An Underworld at War ~ Spivs Deserters Racketeers and Civilians in the Second World War by Donald Thomas. Published by John Murray

The People's War. Britain 1939-1945 by Angus Calder. Published by Jonathon Cape.

Hastings Bygones. Volume 4. Millennium Edition. Published by Hastings Local History Group.

Bombers Over Sussex. 1939-1945 by Pat Burgess and Andy Saunders. Published by Middleton Press.

Letters from Lavender Cottage

by Victoria Seymour

Hastings in WWII and Austerity

A collection of recently discovered letters, posted from Hastings to Canada between 1942 and 1955, inspired Victoria Seymour to compile a part-biography of their writer, Emilie Crane.

In her retirement, Emilie shared a house in Hastings, England, with her two friends, Clare and Edith and their much-loved cat, James. The almost one hundred letters Emilie sent to her Canadian cousins were initially of thanks for the food parcels they had supplied to the Lavender Cottage household in WWII and throughout the following years of harsh austerity. The letters also detail the lively and kind-hearted Emilie Crane's domestic and personal life and follow the joint fortunes of the three ageing women.

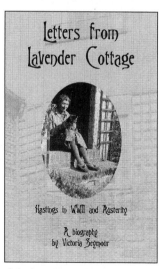

Victoria Seymour has rounded the story by adding contemporary national, local and autobiographical material. "Letters From Lavender Cottage" is a touching, human story with an informative narrative.

ISBN: 0-9543901-0-5   www.victoriaseymour.com

Letters to Hannah

written & compiled by Victoria Seymour

WWII Recollections
of Hastings & South East England

Letters to Hannah looks at WWII on the Home Front through the eyes of those who lived in Hastings and South East England from September 1939 to December 1945. It also enlarges on the historical background covered in its companion book, Letters from Lavender Cottage.

Letters to Hannah visits the lives of ordinary people, who endured extraordinary times. Among many others is the account of a Battle lad, born in a cottage beside the famous 1066 battlefield. Aged fifteen he enlisted as a Home Guard, the youngest member in the country at that time, a Hastings, wartime milk delivery girl details her working and family life under fire and a young first aid volunteer highlights the horrors of bomb and machine gun attacks on civilians. 'Letters to Hannah' is rich in anecdotes and information on food rationing and shortages, the blackout, air raids, population evacuation and civil defence. The book provides a moving and factual account of wartime Hastings, the town which features in the ITV, WWII detective fiction series, Foyle's War.

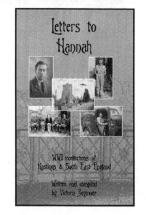

Victoria Seymour links this, her second WWII social history, with a series of autobiographical letters to the future, describing her war-troubled childhood to her newborn, 21st century granddaughter, Hannah. Extracts from Letters to Hannah were included in the BBC Radio 4 history series, The Archive Hour, in July 2003.

ISBN: 0-9543901-1-3   www.victoriaseymour.com